Kidnap of the
FLYING LADY

*"For Cynthia, without whom this book
would not have been possible."*

First published in 2003 by Motorbooks International, an imprint of
MBI Publishing Company, Galtier Plaza, Suite 200, 380 Jackson Street,
St. Paul, MN 55101-3885 USA

The information in this book is true and complete to the best of our
knowledge. All recommendations are made without any guarantee on the
part of the author or Publisher, who also disclaim any liability incurred in
connection with the use of this data or specific details.

We recognise that some words, model names and designations, for example,
mentioned herein are the property of the trademark holder.
We use them for identification purposes only.
This is not an official publication.

Motorbooks International titles are also available at discounts in bulk
quantity for industrial or sales-promotional use. For details write to Special
Sales Manager at Motorbooks International Wholesalers & Distributors,
Galtier Plaza, Suite 200, 380 Jackson Street, St. Paul, MN 55101-3885 USA.

Talk to the publisher about this book:
rob@motorbooksinternational.co.uk

ISBN 0-7603-1686-4

Printed in Hong Kong

Kidnap of the
FLYING
LADY

How Germany Captured both Rolls-Royce & Bentley

Richard Feast

MOTORBOOKS
INTERNATIONAL

CONTENTS

—

CHAPTER 1
THE DIVISION OF THE SPOILS

CHAPTER 2
WHEN ROLLS MET ROYCE

CHAPTER 3
FLYING ALTERS EVERYTHING

CHAPTER 4
PICKING UP THE PIECES POST-WAR

CHAPTER 5
WHEN ROLLS-ROYCE BOUGHT BENTLEY

CHAPTER 6
THE END OF AN ERA

CHAPTER 7
ROLLS-ROYCE GOES TO WAR

CHAPTER 8
A TIME OF CLOUDS AND SHADOWS

CHAPTER 9
DOWN, BUT NOT OUT

CHAPTER 10
ALL CHANGE

CHAPTER 11
BENTLEY COMES IN FROM THE COLD

CHAPTER 12
ONE CRISIS TOO MANY FOR VICKERS

CHAPTER 13
BMW MAKES ITS MARK

CHAPTER 14
THE BRUNEI BONANZA

CHAPTER 15
CREWE CHANGE

CHAPTER 16
MEANWHILE, IN THE OUTSIDE WORLD

CHAPTER 17
VICKERS CHANGES DIRECTION

CHAPTER 18
THE PLAYERS

CHAPTER 19
A COSY COMPETITION

CHAPTER 20
VOLKSWAGEN WINS HALF THE BATTLE

CHAPTER 21
THE TURNING POINT

CHAPTER 22
THE KING IS DEAD. LONG LIVE THE KING

CHAPTER 23
BMW BUILDS A ROLLS-ROYCE

CHAPTER 24
WAS IT WORTH IT?

CHAPTER 1

THE DIVISION OF
THE SPOILS

The scene is the neatly manicured private golf club at Neuen-an-der-Donau in Bavaria, southern Germany, early on the morning of July 28, 1998. The recently risen sun is already beginning to clear the overnight mist and dew lingering on the links. Another lovely summer day is promised. Chauffeur-driven cars whisper into the car park and, to the sound of clunking doors, the actors begin to appear on stage. Sober-looking men in suits, they are clearly not about to play golf. Serious business is afoot involving the biggest names in Germany's motor industry.

Here is Dr Ferdinand Piëch, the immensely wealthy scion of one of the world's great motor industry dynasties and chairman of the board of management of the Volkswagen group. With him are Dr Klaus Liesen, chairman of Volkswagen's supervisory board, and Helmut Schröder, at the time premier of the German province of Lower Saxony, which has a controlling stake in Volkswagen. The Volkswagen delegation is completed by Dr Jens Neumann, Piëch's trusty lieutenant and the management board member responsible for strategy, and Kurt Rippholz, the second in command in the group's public affairs department. They have flown in Volkswagen's Falcon executive jet to the Luftwaffe airfield at nearby Manching, and been wafted to the golf course in a fleet of silver Audi A8s. Liesen has interrupted his vacation for the event, and returns immediately to his villa in Majorca after the morning's brief business is complete.

There is an equally heavyweight team from BMW, led by Dr Bernd Pischetsrieder, the chairman of the board of management, and Dr Eberhard v. Kuenheim, chairman of the supervisory board and the man who, more than any other, was responsible for the creation of the modern BMW group. Not wanting to be out-ranked on the political front, BMW asked the premier of its home state of Bavaria, Edmund Stoiber, to be present. He arrived by helicopter from Munich. Four years later, Schröder and Stoiber were to face each other across the political divide in the electoral battle to become Chancellor of Germany. Completing the BMW team are Dr Hagen Lüderitz, the board's top legal adviser, and Richard Gaul, director of corporate affairs.

The atmosphere in the club house is relaxed but purposeful. Everyone understands the significance of what is about to take place. After haggling for four months, a final agreement has been reached allowing the two German car groups to divide between them the crown jewels of the British motor industry. Volkswagen had already bought Bentley and its assets, but BMW would get Rolls-Royce. In the process, two companies jointly owned since 1931 would be separated. The possibility of adverse reactions in Britain to an event as traumatic as a 2-0 German victory over England on the soccer field was in everyone's mind.

The 10 people are present to sign the legal documents covering the agreement or to act as witnesses. A photographer is briefly summoned to record the event for posterity once the formal signing is complete at about 9am. The party then quickly breaks up. Six of them – Piëch, Neumann and Rippholz, Pischetsrieder, Lüderitz and Gaul – now have another important assignment. They are to fly to London to tell the world what has been decided.

The six pile into the Audi A8s to be taken back to Manching, where they board Volkswagen's waiting Falcon jet for the quick flight to Northolt, a former RAF airfield in north-west London now also used for private aviation. Waiting for the executives at Northolt are four BMW 7-series saloons that take them to a hastily arranged late-morning press briefing at the Institution of Civil Engineers in Great George Street, a few minutes from the Houses of Parliament.

The media had been alerted to the meeting only hours before by Chris Willows, BMW's corporate communications director in the UK. Journalists were told the event would be important, but not what would be announced. It did not take a seer to predict, though. Speculation had been rife throughout the international motor industry since Vickers, the British engineering group that owned Rolls-Royce and Bentley, put the two companies up for sale nine months earlier.

The decision came as a shock because Vickers always insisted that building luxury cars was one of its core businesses. With hindsight, it was simply a sale waiting to happen. Vickers was one of the great pillars of British industry dating back to the 19th century. But it had lost its aircraft and shipbuilding businesses to the nationalisation dogma of the Labour Party of the early 1970s. It merged with Rolls-Royce in 1980, but a series of disposals and acquisitions suggested an ageing dowager in search of a role in the modern, fast-paced world.

News of the Rolls-Royce and Bentley sale immediately generated expressions of interest from a string of hopeful enthusiasts. At best, they were distractions. Vickers went through the motions of listening, but it was clear that only serious and substantial automotive groups need apply. Vickers could not be seen by the public to sell such highly emotive assets to any private consortium – however well-meaning – that did not already have the specialist knowledge, finances, technology and global structure to develop the two brands.

Vickers also needed to make a successful disposal of Rolls-Royce and Bentley for the benefit of its shareholders. It did. Bidding was finally reduced to two players, Volkswagen and BMW. After weeks of corporate posturing, Volkswagen triumphed with an offer of £430 million. It did so by matching the terms earlier agreed by Vickers and BMW, and then adding another £90 million to the offer price. To underline its seriousness, Volkswagen agreed to purchase Cosworth Engineering, another Vickers company, for £117 million. Vickers had paid over £163 million for Cosworth just eight years earlier.

However, the price Vickers achieved for Rolls-Royce and Bentley was even more impressive, for two main reasons.

First, the waiting media gathered in London was about to discover that Volkswagen's offer had bought it Bentley, the Rolls-Royce factory and workforce at Crewe, and the car maker's global distribution structure. But the deal included only the temporary rights to use what is unquestionably one of the world's great automotive iconic names, Rolls-Royce. Separately, BMW had negotiated to use the Rolls-Royce brand on passenger cars and would assert its permanent ownership from January 2003. The development was effectively formulated years earlier in a cosy little arrangement between Pischetsrieder of BMW and Sir Ralph Robins, the chairman of Rolls-Royce plc. Had anyone at Volkswagen really understood the implications of that alliance, it is doubtful whether the offer would have been quite so large.

To understand what lay behind the alliance it is necessary to go back to the collapse of Rolls-Royce in 1971. The bankruptcy was the biggest the country had ever experienced. The psychological damage to Britain was enormous. For decades Rolls-Royce had been a source of national pride and admired around the world for its technological expertise in aircraft engine design and manufacturing. The problems suffered by Rolls-Royce were not associated with its car-manufacturing side, which was just about profitable. They arose because of a contract to develop a new generation of giant turbofan engines for wide-body airliners. The RB-211 engine's pioneering technology did not initially work, the project fell behind schedule, and there were punitive penalty clauses in the key contract with Lockheed, the US aerospace company which was trying to market the L-1011 airliner, known later as the TriStar.

Eventually Rolls-Royce was forced to call in the receivers. By that time the construction of Rolls-Royce and Bentley cars comprised barely 5 per cent of group revenues. But as a profitable unit, it was split off and in 1973 floated on the London Stock Exchange as Rolls-Royce Motors. Such was the lack of understanding about the value of brands at the time that no car maker even bothered to take a small strategic stake in the new company, though one of the holding companies that controls the interests of Fiat's Agnelli family bought a shareholding.

With a share price of 90 pence, the market valued Rolls-Royce Motors and its manufacturing assets at £30 million. It is quite a contrast to the £430 million Volkswagen would pay 25 years later for a marginally profitable company susceptible to huge losses in periods of low demand. Even by the time Rolls-Royce Motors merged with Vickers in 1980, the former's share price was down to 61 pence.

As a major defence contractor, and in deference to the political mood of the time, the aero engine side of Rolls-Royce was nationalised. It was subsequently privatised when the free market economics of the Conservative Party under Margaret Thatcher set the political agenda. Throughout it all, though, Aerospace held the legal rights to who could use the Rolls-Royce name, even on products made by another company. It was effectively a protective golden share to prevent the name being used by a foreign manufacturer. So, while permission was willingly granted to a fine, upstanding British company like Vickers, what would happen when Vickers embarked on a new strategy by trying to sell Rolls-Royce Motors? On the face of it, Vickers appeared to be offering for sale something it did not own.

The situation was not clear to Vickers, which took legal advice to determine the Rolls-Royce ownership rights. Vickers knew it owned Bentley, and believed it owned Rolls-Royce. Neither was the issue clear to the rest of the world, including the financial community. However, Robins at Rolls-Royce plc was in no doubt about how he could use his veto over what was a separate company. Neither was Pischetsrieder at BMW. It was to prove an unbeatable combination.

The two had come to know each other in the early 1990s when they formed a joint venture to develop and build small turbofan engines for feeder airliners. The second leg of Pischetsrieder's strategy emerged in 1994 when BMW beat Mercedes-Benz in a competition to supply critical engine technology for a new generation of cars planned for Rolls-Royce and Bentley.

But exactly how Rolls-Royce and Bentley managed to fund this joint programme is perhaps the most extraordinary, and certainly least-known, episode in the histories of both companies. It developed after the economic downturn at the start of the 1990s saw world demand for top luxury cars plummet. When losses at Rolls-Royce and its Bentley subsidiary mounted to £1 million a week, the company was forced to make painful cuts simply to keep afloat.

Sales eventually recovered, but the experience underlined the need to modernise the model range. By 1994, when the technology supply agreement with BMW was forged, the basic designs of the Silver Shadow and Mulsanne models dated back to 1965. True, they were improved and developed during that time. But over three decades the cars from Crewe had in effect slipped three generations behind their competitors – notably Mercedes-Benz and BMW – in terms of technology, refinement, emissions, economy and packaging. It was increasingly hard to justify the price premium demanded for a Rolls-Royce or Bentley.

However, the grand old names still retained their aura of understated superiority. As national economies revived, so loyal customers gradually returned, to the point where Rolls-Royce was again marginally profitable. Sales of its regular models made the manufacturer self-funding at an operating level, but it could not generate enough cash to fund development costs for the desperately needed new generation of cars to which it was committed. And Vickers, the parent group, was not prepared to pay for the new models after underwriting the car maker so substantially at the beginning of the decade.

Salvation for Rolls-Royce and Bentley came from an unlikely source: a playboy prince from the tiny, oil-rich Sultanate of Brunei with its population of barely 300,000. "Fabulously wealthy" barely describes Prince Jefri, brother of the sultan and at the time the country's finance minister. Jefri was an Olympic gold medal winner several times over in the freestyle spending stakes. And Jefri absolutely adored expensive, exclusive cars. He bought hundreds of Ferraris, Porsches, Aston Martins, Brabus-tuned Mercedes-Benz and McLarens. But his particular love was for British cars in general, and Bentleys in particular. And not just any Bentley. He commissioned unique, one-off Bentleys at £1 million each – give or take a few hundred thousand pounds – and then ordered them by the half-dozen.

The prince was later sued by the sultan for misappropriating state funds. Many of Jefri's hugely costly baubles were auctioned in order to settle some of the debts, but the thousands of cars acquired during his uncontrolled spending binge were not among them. Certain Brunei cars are occasionally dribbled on to the secondhand market, but for the most part they are, apparently, still guarded by Ghurka troops in four air-conditioned warehouses within the sprawling grounds of the 1,788-room royal palace in Bandar Seri Begawan, the capital of Brunei. Their value today is impossible to estimate.

Prince Jefri was spending perhaps £150 million a year on Bentleys, and to a lesser extent Rolls-Royces, from 1994 to early 1997. His elder brother also has an enviable collection. This spending by the Brunei royal family proved to be the company's salvation. Rolls-Royce was paying its way through normal sales of cars, but the flow of funds from Brunei effectively underwrote the cost of developing the Silver Seraph and Arnage models and the re-organisation of the Crewe factory in order to manufacture them.

To bring those two new cars to market, BMW set about making itself indispensable to Rolls-Royce Motors as a technology supplier. At the same time, it fostered the relationship with Rolls-Royce plc through the aircraft engine joint venture. By the time the future of Rolls-Royce as a car maker came up for grabs, the outcome was virtually a done deal as far as Robins and Pischetsrieder were concerned. The BMW man simply threatened that if Volkswagen acquired Rolls-Royce and Bentley, BMW would cut its technology supply agreement after one year, as it was entitled to under the terms of the agreement forged when Vickers was owner of the car companies. In a business in which development lead times are measured in years, Volkswagen would have the names, but no new products to sell for three or four years.

It was a classic check-mate by a grand strategist who had planned his moves over several years. Pischetsrieder really wanted both companies, but knew he would be able to acquire Rolls-Royce whatever happened. When Volkswagen paid what he considered too high a price, Pischetsrieder simply struck a deal with Robins to buy the car-making rights to Rolls-Royce for £40 million, and nothing more. Vickers got nothing from BMW. While some of Piëch's colleagues wanted Volkswagen to get both marques, the chairman took the decision from the beginning that he was only really interested in Bentley. Under the circumstances, he was satisfied with the deal, though few outside his close circle really believed it. In addition to Bentley, Volkswagen was granted the rights to use the Rolls-Royce brand for the following 53 months. That would give BMW time to design and develop a new model, build a factory in which to make it, and recruit a workforce.

Such was the unusual deal outlined at the media briefing in London by the three central characters, Pischetsrieder, Piëch and Robins. Significantly, it was the first time Piëch and Robins had met. It was indicative of Volkswagen's intent that negotiations with Rolls-Royce plc over the car use of the Rolls-Royce name were led by Dr Robert Büchelhofer, then Volkswagen's board member responsible for sales and marketing. The company did not judge that, to break the strength of the bond between Pischetsrieder and Robins, it might require the intervention of Piëch as chairman.

Tellingly, no one from Vickers was present.

Willows, the UK BMW executive whose office organised the meeting, was asked to act as moderator. It was a shrewd move. Willows' clearly English tone served to emphasise the 'Britishness' of BMW, which at that stage still owned the Rover group; the sell-off would not come for nearly another year. Willows first introduced the silver-haired Robins, a distinguished-looking gentleman who could easily fit central casting's definition of a British business establishment character. After a brief statement from Robins, Willows introduced the affable Pischetsrieder, who was totally comfortable in the English language following a seven-year spell in South Africa. Those language skills were honed at Rover, and also in the United States, where Pischetsrieder led the BMW team that secretly searched for a suitable site for the firm's first transplant factory.

Then it was Piëch's turn. Piëch is one of the world's over-achievers, an internationally admired Austrian who transformed the products of the Volkswagen group. But brilliant engineer and businessman though he is, Piëch is not the most approachable character. Those who have met him talk of a remote and seemingly taciturn manner in which conversations are punctuated by cold silences. His English is slow and heavily accented.

In this environment, in which all the other main characters spoke fluent English, Piëch was uncomfortable, and it showed. He was not just handicapped by language. The Volkswagen delegation was irked when it learned that a live satellite TV link had been arranged to allow German journalists to ask questions. In itself, that was not a problem. It was the fact that they were sitting in BMW's headquarters building in Munich, not one at Volkswagen in Wolfsburg, or even one in a neutral location.

Questions from the floor came thick and fast after the formal statements. The details of the unprecedented deal slowly sank in, but the headline, on the face of it, was that Volkswagen had paid £430 million for the lesser-known Bentley brand and BMW paid £40 million for the epitome of all car-making brands, Rolls-Royce. It was this apparent absurdity that provoked a damning question from a German journalist. For Willows, a BMW employee and the sole conduit for questions to the panellists from Munich, it proved the low point in his career. "Dr Piëch," he was obliged to repeat, "Don't you think you've made a fool of yourself?"

The question-and-answer session was wound up after about 90 minutes, but even then the scrum spilled out on to the pavement outside where the BMW 7-series were waiting to take the BMW and Volkswagen executives back to Northolt. While both sides declared themselves pleased with the compromise, one person was totally elated: Pischetsrieder. "This is the best day of my life," he confided to colleagues. "It has secured the strategy for the group." He was on a high as he settled into the back of the 7-series, puffing a fat cigar. No one felt it appropriate to remind the chairman that BMW (Great

Britain) operates a no-smoking policy for its company cars.

The Falcon first flew to Wolfsburg, where the Volkswagen delegation departed, and then on to Manching to take the BMW party back to Bavaria. For the first part of the flight, they were joined by Graham Morris, the chief executive of Rolls-Royce and Bentley in Crewe. He was on his way to Wolfsburg for a scheduled presentation to the Volkswagen strategy board the following day about the future of Rolls-Royce and Bentley, a presentation that the day's events had suddenly rendered pointless. Morris already knew Piëch quite well. Before joining Rolls-Royce in March 1997, Piëch had recruited him to be the board member for sales and marketing at Audi, Volkswagen's upmarket car maker.

Morris was distressed by the prospect of the Rolls-Royce/Bentley break-up. He had always promised the employees at Crewe that it would not happen. His mind virtually made up to resign, Morris felt no compunction in asking Piëch a direct question. Why had the chairman referred to Rolls-Royce's Spirit of Ecstasy statue as "Emely" in the press conference? No one knew what Piëch was talking about, because the German nickname for the famous emblem is totally unknown outside that country. The expression suggested a mis-reading of the Rolls-Royce character and the issues involved.

While Piëch may not have known about "Emely", he wholly understood the implications of Rolls-Royce plc's historical hold over the nameplate. He was also familiar with the business relationship between Pischetsrieder and Robins through the aircraft engine joint venture. He knew because ever since the Vickers-Volkswagen bid was agreed, he had held top secret meetings with Pischetsrieder every Monday in order to iron out the details involved in the division of the spoils. The mystery was why Piëch did not also try to establish an agreement with Robins, chairman to chairman, over the use of the name rather than delegate the task to Büchelhofer.

The real surprise for Piëch, which he acknowledged in the press conference, was the degree to which BMW, along with its suppliers, were such integral parts of the Silver Seraph and Arnage. It went beyond the engines and transmissions that everyone knew about to include other critical elements like the air conditioning, suspension systems and the electronics that control everything in the cars. Getting BMW components into Rolls-Royce was part of Pischetsrieder's long-term strategy to secure the marque.

For Piëch then to call the Spirit of Ecstasy "Emely" suggested a Volkswagen remoteness from the true situation concerning Rolls-Royce. Piëch's accented and faltering English, in contrast to the fluency of his fellow panel members, merely compounded his problems. His smile for the obligatory handshake photographs with Pischetsrieder and Robins looked strained. Piëch's appearance was that of a man who knew he had been out-manoeuvred.

The deals done, the two German car makers immediately began intensive product development programmes resulting in the launch of the Bentley Continental GT at the Paris motor show in October 2002 and the Rolls-Royce Phantom at the motor show in Detroit three months later. The first reactions were that both companies had successfully returned to their distinctive roots: Bentley as a maker of rather louche, high-performance luxury cars and Rolls-Royce as a producer of supremely dignified limousines suitable for the most presidential posterior. But that is not the end of the story, or even the new beginning. Between the events of the summer of 1998 and the launch of the new models, there were further dramas involving the various companies and the people who ran them.

Barely six months after basking in the "best moment of my career", Bernd Pischetsrieder was fired as chairman of BMW. The reason had nothing to do with Rolls-Royce, and everything to do with the financial problems at the Rover group. In a surprise move in February 1994, BMW bought the British group as a means of increasing its scale and broadening its market appeal. But continuing heavy losses at Rover, compounded by the strength of sterling and falling sales, dragged down the overall performance of the BMW group. Pischetsrieder, the man who bought Rover only nine months after becoming chairman, had to go. And so did Rover. BMW retained its Mini project, but sold Land Rover to Ford and the MG

Rover passenger car business to a private consortium. Once it did so, BMW's business performance once more became one of the best in the automotive sector.

By a curious twist of fate, Pischetsrieder was subsequently hired by Piëch, whom he replaced when the latter retired in 2002. As chairman of Volkswagen, Pischetsrieder thus became responsible for the brand he declared at the time was not his priority – Bentley.

BMW's return to the aero engine sector through the joint venture with Rolls-Royce plc was a commercial failure. While the development of the engine itself was successful, the market for the type of short-haul, feeder airliner for which it was intended did not develop. As a result, BMW swapped its aircraft engine assets – most of them in Germany – for a 10 per cent shareholding in Rolls-Royce plc.

Ostensibly, the reason for Vickers selling its Rolls-Royce and Bentley car businesses, as well as Cosworth Engineering, was to concentrate its resources on its other main sectors, battle tanks and marine propulsion. It did not happen. In September 1999, Rolls-Royce plc bought the remains of Vickers. Three years later, it sold the tank business to Alvis, but retained the marine propulsion operations.

So, the German executive who wanted to buy one British prestige car maker is in charge of the one he failed to acquire. Vickers, the owner of Rolls-Royce and Bentley for 18 years and a pillar of Britain's proud engineering heritage, no longer exists as an independent company. Rolls-Royce, the car maker, is part of BMW, which is the largest industrial shareholder in Rolls-Royce plc. And Bentley, for so long the neglected orphan of Rolls-Royce, is in the charge of a company established in the 1930s to provide an economical People's Car for Germany. Truth, as ever, can be stranger than fiction.

CHAPTER 2

WHEN ROLLS MET ROYCE

The world, and Britain's role in it, was very different just over a century ago. When the founders of what became Rolls-Royce and Bentley were born, the British Empire was at its peak, covering a quarter of the globe. When Queen Victoria's Golden Jubilee was celebrated in 1887, the year after she was named Empress of India, Rolls was just 10 years old and Royce was 24. Bentley was born the following year.

Britannia may have ruled the waves, but the vision, greed and spirit of adventure that created the Empire were lacking when the car was in its infancy. This absence was even more surprising for a nation responsible for generating the industrial revolution. Steam power, smelting, railways, iron and steel making, machine tools, textiles, electric motors and the telegraph were all perfected in Britain and operated commercially around the world. Yet the development of road vehicles, which were destined to revolutionise transport, was initially almost ignored in Britain. It was German, French and American entrepreneurs who pioneered the development of motoring.

Enthusiasm for any parallel enterprises in Britain was dampened by the infamous Red Flag Act of 1865. This required road vehicles to be preceded by a person on foot carrying a red flag and restricted speeds to 2 mph in towns and 4 mph in the countryside. While the flag was subsequently dispensed with, the person in front of the vehicle was not. This capitulation to the country's highly influential railway interests and to the lobbying of the horse establishment demonstrated a blindness to any economic and social benefits that might stem from the creation of an entirely new manufacturing sector. The hated Act was eventually rescinded in 1896, but only in part: speed was still limited to 12 mph.

By that time, motorised Daimler and Benz vehicles had already been on the roads for a decade. Shortly after, Panhard et Levassor and Peugeot in France took out licences to build cars to Daimler designs. In 1893, the Duryea brothers built a motorised buggy that is generally accepted to be America's first practical car. It was not long before other American inventors such as Henry Ford and Ransom E. Olds were testing their own experimental vehicles. By the early 20th century, there were hundreds of hopeful (and hopeless) car producers, most of which did not survive. A century later, a similar situation characterised the booming information technology industry.

The motoring pioneers eventually changed the world, though the democratisation of mobility had to wait until the arrival of mass production in the 1920s. Early motoring was the preserve of the wealthy because the first cars were hand-built by craftsmen. The work was frequently unscientific. New technologies, new methods of construction and new materials meant slow fabrication by trial and error. Thus, all cars were expensive, and some more so than others. This, then, was the late Victorian Britain that shaped the thinking and actions of the founders of Rolls-Royce and Bentley.

The background of the Hon. Charles Stewart Rolls did not mark him out as an obvious motoring pioneer in Britain. The third son of a baronet, he was born in London's elite Mayfair district in 1877 and educated at Eton (as were his father and brothers) and at Trinity College, Cambridge. But while most young men of his era studied the dead civilisations of Rome and Greece, Rolls's degree was in mechanics and applied science.

In Rolls' world of *Upstairs-Downstairs*, the children of wealthy landowners did not traditionally enter the vulgar domain of trade or commerce. Law, politics, the clergy, and the Army were more likely callings for gentlemen. Charlie Rolls was different. After graduation, he worked as an engineer on the family's steam yacht and later studied in the workshops of the great railway centre of Crewe, a town that in the second half of the 20th century became synonymous with the production of Rolls-Royce and Bentley cars.

To say that Rolls was fascinated by everything mechanical and electrical is an understatement. He was interested in very little else. Even as a student, he had installed electricity in part of the family's country estate, the Hendre, in Monmouthshire. At Cambridge, he represented the university in the then fashionable sport of cycle racing. By that stage, though, he had already discovered the appeal of motoring on a visit to France. He embraced it totally, until it was overtaken by an obsession for aviation that led to his early death.

Rolls' first car was a Peugeot Phaeton imported from France to England, where it was used on gruelling journeys between London, Cambridge and Monmouthshire. The appeal is difficult to comprehend today, given the primitive nature of the car, the existence of speed limits, the state of the roads, and the efficiency of the railways at the time. But Rolls was a driven man and a determined motoring pioneer. He was a founder member of the Automobile Club (the Royal prefix came later) and strong campaigner for the repeal of the Red Flag Act. He competed successfully in numerous reliability trials, including the 1900 London to Edinburgh event in which he won an Automobile Club gold medal driving a Panhard.

Although Rolls was wealthy, there was still a problem in funding his extravagant motoring activity. There was no hint of the champagne and night-club lifestyle embraced by many young bloods in the later Victorian era. On the contrary, Rolls was notorious for his parsimony. He would travel second or third class while his peers inevitably went first. His wardrobe was spare. Rolls was even known to take his own sandwiches into the Automobile Club dining room and ask for water to accompany them, until the club imposed a service charge of a few pence.

In 1902, using money advanced by his father, Rolls established C.S. Rolls & Co., based in London's Lillie Hall, Fulham. Its purpose was to sell cars imported from Continental Europe, mainly Panhard et Levassors, to his wealthy friends.

Another event that would have a profound effect on Rolls came the following year. In December 1903, the Wright brothers made their first powered flight in North Carolina. Flying, even more than cars, was to become the fatal passion of Rolls' life.

Rolls had recruited Claude Johnson, the well-connected secretary of the Automobile Club, to run the car operation. But while Rolls and Johnson had all the right contacts, the venture was not a great success. The turning point came when Rolls investigated a new car being built in Manchester by an electrical company called Royce.

Frederick Henry Royce came from the other end of the social spectrum. Born in 1863, he was the fifth child of a miller in the town of Alwalton, now part of the conurbation around Peterborough. When Royce Senior's business failed, he took the family to London. Young Fred's education was cut short after his father died in penury at only 41. Royce had to work to help support the family, which he did by selling newspapers for W.H. Smith at Clapham Junction and Bishopsgate. He was able to return to school briefly, but by the age of 12 was a telegraph messenger in a Mayfair post office.

However, an aunt took pity on the boy. She paid £20 a year for him to become an apprentice at the Great Northern Railway works at Peterborough. She additionally paid for his lodgings with the Yarrow family. It was a fortuitous development, for his landlord was a skilled fitter and machinist. What Royce did not learn at work, he picked up in Yarrow's garden shed.

But Royce was unable to complete his apprenticeship after his aunt ran into financial difficulties. Armed with testimonials from his supervisor, Royce, aged 16, tramped north to Leeds and Bradford in search of work. It was a difficult period, because employees were being laid off rather than taken on. He eventually landed work as a tool maker in Leeds at 11 shillings (55 pence) for a 54-hour week. In what little spare time remained, Royce began to learn all he could about the new science of electricity. The workaholic, obsessive nature of Royce's later years was becoming apparent.

He became a tester at London's Light and Power Company, and

was later seconded to its affiliated electrical company in Liverpool. Both firms eventually failed, but not before Royce had gained a deep understanding of the nature of electricity, then still in its infancy. With his engineering knowledge, and a little capital he had saved, and still only 21 years old, Royce felt confident enough to start his own electrical engineering business.

Royce's partner was a fellow electrical engineer and friend, Ernest Claremont. They were also brothers-in-law, having married the daughters of Alfred Punt, Minnie and Edith respectively. With electric lighting beginning to replace gas lamps on the streets of the country's towns and villages, it was an auspicious moment to launch the new venture.

The company, initially known as F.H. Royce & Co. and later Royce & Co., was based in Manchester and made electric light fittings. It subsequently graduated to electric motors, dynamos and switch gear. These found ready buyers in the mining and textile industries. By the end of the century, Royce was making electrical cranes and hoists that removed a lot of the hard, physical labour in the nation's steel mills, railway yards and docksides – and on the Manchester Ship Canal then under construction. Already, the exacting standards that were to become familiar in the motor cars he later designed were present in Royce's cranes: they were durable, quiet and expensive. It was an early indication of what was to become one of Royce's famous aphorisms: that the quality remains long after the price has been forgotten.

The business provided Royce with a comfortable living, and he was able to move to a large house in Knutsford, about 15 miles from the Cooke Street factory in Manchester. But the effects of the Boer War (1899-1902) and international competition from the United States and Germany saw a slump in demand for Royce products. It was therefore no surprise that an enquiring engineer like Royce would turn his attention to other opportunities. It was a time when the new-fangled motor cars were beginning to appear on the roads around Manchester. After buying a French Decauville, it was not long before Royce decided it could be improved on. Against the opposition of his fellow directors, Royce decided in 1903 to build three cars of his own.

The first car, completed in the spring of 1904, was a two-cylinder 10 HP. It broke no new technical ground, but, in an era when cars were fragile and unreliable, it bore the Royce stamp of refinement and perfection. The very creation of a car from scratch was an achievement in itself at the time. Like all cars in that pioneering period, virtually everything in the Royce was fabricated in-house. The design of every component, every calculation, was done by Royce himself. The components manufacturing industry had not yet developed. Even when it had, Royce's instinct told him no supplier could match his own standards. While the philosophy was gradually eased after Royce's death, Rolls-Royce was still making its own nuts and bolts up to the 1980s, at a time when GKN was able to sell the same items at a fraction of the price.

What was to become one of the most famous meetings in motoring history took place about a month after the first Royce appeared. It was instigated by Henry Edmunds, an entrepreneur, investor and early motoring enthusiast who told his friend Charles Rolls about the new Royce motor car being made in Manchester. Rolls was looking for a British vehicle, rather than French ones, to sell through his recently established London showroom. Although he may not have known it at the time, if Royce was to develop the motor car side of his business, he needed a well-connected person who could mastermind the advertising and sales side.

Rolls travelled to Manchester to meet Royce at the Midland Hotel on May 4, 1904. The meeting was a success. Rolls liked the man and his car, even though it was a two-cylinder and not the four-cylinder he wanted. Royce liked the young Rolls. Fourteen years his junior and from a different social background, Rolls was a fellow traveller because he was an engineer.

The final agreement that created the Rolls-Royce partnership was signed in December. Royce would make the cars, and Rolls would sell them. The utilitarian and functional Royce radiator was abandoned after only a handful of cars were made, replaced by the radiator – and much later by a radiator grille – that would come to symbolise Rolls-Royce cars.

A formal Rolls-Royce company, incorporating most of the assets of C.S. Rolls & Co. and Royce Co., was not registered until March 1906. However, the company that made some of the finest cars in the world was consistently short of money. It had grand plans for a new range of cars, but it needed a new factory in which to build them and modern machine tools to do the job. A £50,000 public flotation was organised to provide the necessary capital for the company's future. But investors were wary of motor businesses. There were too many of them and the prospects of reward were too vague. The Rolls-Royce issue, despite substantial support by Rolls himself, was under-subscribed. The episode provided a foretaste of developments a century later, when initial enthusiasm for dotcom share flotations quickly gave way to almost total scepticism.

The situation was saved only by a cheque for £10,000 from Arthur Briggs, a wealthy Yorkshire businessman as well as a Rolls-Royce owner and motoring enthusiast. The investment assured Briggs a place on the board of Rolls-Royce until his death in 1919, an event that prompted the company to bind its annual report in black that year.

During those early years, Rolls promoted the new cars at exhibitions and in competitions in the United Kingdom, France and the United States. Claude Johnson proved an admirable administrator and organiser in Rolls's absence, including overseeing the opening of a new showroom in London's fashionable Conduit Street. Royce, meanwhile, was busy designing models of three, four and six cylinders. There was even a V8. More importantly, though, he was working on the design of a model that would cement Rolls-Royce's reputation among the car cognoscenti. It was the company's answer to the models being produced by Napier, then one of the leading top-quality car manufacturers.

The model was the six-cylinder 40/50 HP, first seen at the Olympia exhibition in London in 1906. Later known as the Silver Ghost – because of its polished aluminium bodywork – it was to become the cornerstone of the company's one-model policy for the next two decades. It was Royce's uncompromising masterpiece, the model that earned the company the reputation for building "the best car in the world". It was an appellation that lingered in the public perception long after the company's products no longer justified the description towards the end of the century.

While a few early 40/50s were assembled in Manchester, a priority for the newly formed company was to determine where to establish a new factory for series production. Various local authorities competed for the award because of the jobs it would create and the wealth that would flow into the local economy. Derby finally won with the offer of a 5.1 hectare site on Nightingale Road, together with the incentives of low business rates and electricity charges. It was to prove a fortuitous agreement for the town. While car production was moved to Crewe after the Second World War, the Rolls-Royce aero engine business is still a major presence in the town. Ironically, aircraft engines were not part of Rolls-Royce activities at the time, although they shortly would be.

The factory was formally opened in July 1908 by Sir John (later Lord) Montagu. It produced most of the almost 7,900 Silver Ghosts ever made, though some were made in Manchester and others at a factory in Springfield, Massachusetts, from 1920-26.

> *That same year, on August 12, 1908, the first new car of a totally different type was produced in Detroit: the Ford Model T that was to revolutionise motoring in the United States, as well as the manner in which cars are made. The simple, cheap and durable Model T was manufactured on the moving production line, signalling the demise of craft-built production of all but the most expensive cars such as Rolls-Royces.*

The car itself set new standards in refinement, durability and speed. Johnson's flair for publicity saw the model's qualities successfully demonstrated by winning events like the Tourist Trophy in the Isle of Man, the Austrian Alpine Trial and Scottish six-day event. A Silver

Ghost achieved a record non-stop endurance run of 15,000 miles by being driven by a team of drivers between London and Edinburgh. With a new body, the same car was then able to lap the Brooklands motor racing circuit south-west of London at over 100 mph.

The Silver Ghost episode is a telling reminder that many of the issues faced by the motor industry in the early 21st century are not entirely new. Others will appear as Rolls-Royce's history unfolds. To achieve economies of scale (the term is relative), the company dropped a multi-model policy in favour of a single, superior model, the 40/50. To build it, Rolls-Royce wanted a greenfield site and played competing local authorities against each other for the best deal. To demonstrate the Silver Ghost's qualities, cars successfully won the top motor-sporting events of their day. And to sell cars more effectively in the world's largest car market, the United States, it elected to build them there. Today's Japanese and European transplant factories in the United States have their roots in the Rolls-Royce venture in Springfield.

Though only a few years old, Rolls-Royce was at the pinnacle of its early achievements thanks to the Silver Ghost and the people who created it. However, serious issues revolving around the two eponymous founders were about to turn the new company inside out. They did so against a background of growing political dissent in Russia and a German military build-up.

CHAPTER 3

FLYING ALTERS EVERYTHING

With the Silver Ghost a technical and sales success, and an all-new factory capable of manufacturing the model to the exacting Rolls-Royce standards, the company's future looked assured. But the period was also an ominous one for Rolls-Royce. Events were to mark the end of an era for Europe. Britain's Edwardian period closed in May 1910 with the death of Edward VII. The crowned heads of Europe who gathered in London for the funeral would shortly be involved in a conflict that re-shaped the political map of the continent. A few weeks later, on July 12, Charles Rolls was killed in a flying accident. Flying was then such a nascent adventure that he was the first Englishman to die in what *The Times* described as a "motor-driven flying machine". He was only the tenth person in the world to have met the same fate.

Rolls was only 32. However, his society contacts, combined with Claude Johnson's organisational flair and Royce's unbending pursuit of engineering perfection, meant the company had achieved a great deal in a short time. Rolls-Royce had helped to make the dashing young Rolls a household name, but it was his flying activities which cemented his fame. Only five weeks before his death, Rolls became the first person to fly both ways across the English Channel, less than a year after Louis Blériot made the first one-way crossing. The event earned Rolls national acclaim, a place in London's famous Madame Tussaud waxworks, and a congratulatory telegram from the newly crowned King George V.

Rolls, the aristocratic, restless adventurer, could well have been the inspiration for Kenneth Grahame's Mr Toad in *The Wind in the Willows*, first published in 1908. Rolls, like the capricious Mr Toad, was captivated by new concepts of transport, old interests fading as new ones gathered momentum. When Rolls learned the Wright brothers had first taken to the air at the end of 1903, he was determined to meet them during a Rolls-Royce promotional tour in the United States. He was subsequently their host when they visited the UK. Rolls learned to fly, and bought a Wright Flyer, which was built under licence by the Short brothers. This was the aircraft in which Rolls achieved his historic return trip from England to France. It was also the machine, with a modified tailplane, he took to the fateful flying exhibition in Bournemouth.

Watched by thousands of spectators on a blustery day, Rolls was taking part in a competition called the "alighting prize". But, about 30 feet in the air, the modified tailplane broke up and the aircraft plunged nose-first into the ground. Rolls died virtually instantaneously.

Rolls' partnership with Royce was barely six years old. The fact that the company endured, and even thrived after his death, was in large measure attributable to the reliable and efficient Johnson. When Rolls's time-consuming obsession with flying meant he frequently missed meetings, Johnson deftly steered the company and Royce was master of the drawing boards.

That next year, 1911, saw the first appearance of what became shorthand for all that Rolls-Royce represented: the radiator statue known as the Spirit of Ecstasy. The company was concerned by what it regarded as wholly unsuitable radiator ornaments fitted by some of its customers. It therefore commissioned a more appropriate statue from a well-known sculptor of the time, Charles Sykes, and offered it as an option – at extra cost – to clients. The statue, which quickly became one of the company's most powerful promotional images, was said to be modelled on Eleanor Thornton. She was an employee of Claude Johnson during his tenure at the Automobile Club, and by 1911 was secretary to Sir John Montagu, owner of *The Car Illustrated.*

The hand of Johnson was also evident in that other famous symbol of Rolls-Royce cars, the Greek-style radiator and radiator grille. As an engineer, Royce wanted to move on from what he saw as an old-fashioned piece of design. As a publicist, Johnson instinctively knew the value of the distinctive face of Rolls-Royce. For once, Royce bowed to the advice of his trusted colleague.

The first decade of the 20th century saw a flurry of new car companies enter the market. They included Lanchester, Austin and Rover in England, Lancia in Italy, Bugatti in France and Ford in the United States. The group that was to become the largest of them all – General Motors in the United States – was put together by William C. Durant during that period.

However, Royce's health was deteriorating. A combination of long working hours, lack of exercise, and neglect of his nutritional requirements meant that by 1911 he was in serious need of rest and recuperation. Just how serious can be judged by the fact that the obsessional Royce, a man who needed to do everything himself, was persuaded by Johnson to take a winter holiday in Egypt. Returning by car through Italy and France, the two men fell in love with a then-undeveloped part of the Cote d'Azur near Le Canadel. The experience was to change Royce's life.

The mild winter climate of the south of France was judged ideal for a person of his delicate health. A tract of land was purchased at Le Canadel, where the Villa Mimosa was built for Royce (to his own specifications, of course) as well as a drawing office and another villa for visiting designers and engineers. Johnson, too, had a house in the same area.

The pattern was set for the rest of Royce's life. He only visited the factory in Derby once more. With the exception of the war years, winters were spent in the south of France and summers at various houses in the south of England. Royce lived in Crowborough, Sussex, and later at St Margaret's Bay, Kent, but from 1917 his main home in

England was Elmstead in West Wittering, Sussex. This association with Sussex was said to be one of the reasons why BMW elected to establish the headquarters and factory of Rolls-Royce at nearby Goodwood after it bought the marque in the late 1990s.

Health permitting, and freed from the day-to-day decision-making within the manufacturing works, Royce worked constantly, whether he was in the south of France or Sussex. And, it has to be said, Rolls-Royce thrived without the constant engineering interference and unrealistic demands of the company's co-founder. In today's parlance, Royce lacked "people skills". A constant stream of visitors from the works in Derby or from the head office in Conduit Street, London, reassured Royce that he remained at the centre of the enterprise. Meanwhile, the company recruited a number of well-qualified designers, draftsmen and engineers capable of turning the master's instructions into metal.

The key figure in Royce's personal life after his illness was his nurse, Ethel Aubin. Minnie, Royce's wife, did not care for the constant travel, and was said to be uninterested in the physical side of marriage. Indeed, the frigidity of his home life may have been one of the reasons Royce threw himself so whole-heartedly into his work. After his illness and operations, Royce needed the constant care, and companionship, given him by Nurse Aubin for the rest of his life. He appears to have separated from Minnie at around the outbreak of war, though he continued to provide for her.

Ford commissioned the world's first moving production line to manufacture Model Ts at a purpose-built factory in Highland Park, Michigan, in 1913. To recruit enough employees, Henry Ford shortly afterwards offered a wage of $5 a day. Such unprecedented riches caused mass migration from America's southern states.

However, the world was changing, and Rolls-Royce would have to follow. Russia, humiliated by military defeat at the hands of Japan in 1905, was in revolutionary ferment. Germany, recently unified, was creating a formidable military presence in Europe and on the high seas under Kaiser Wilhelm, cousin to Britain's George V. Women's suffrage and Irish home rule were hugely divisive issues in London. And when the Balkans crisis resulted in the assassination of Archduke Franz Ferdinand, the heir to the throne of the Austro-Hungarian Empire, in Sarajevo on June 28, 1914, Europe rapidly descended into war.

The implications for a manufacturer of expensive prestige cars such as Rolls-Royce were profound. Orders suddenly disappeared, leaving the company with many unsold chassis and a very uncertain future. Some Silver Ghost chassis were turned into staff cars for military top brass. They were used with utter reliability at home and in most theatres of the war. Others became ambulances and armoured cars, most famously used by T.E. Lawrence, more popularly known as Lawrence of Arabia. In *The Seven Pillars of Wisdom*, Lawrence described the performance of his Rolls-Royces in the desert as being more valuable than rubies.

But the absence of work meant Rolls-Royce was forced to make many staff at Derby redundant and to reduce wages. The company acquired some light engineering sub-contract work, including assembling Renault-designed V8 engines for Royal Flying Corps aircraft. It was not ideal work – especially as Royce was dismissive of the Renault design – but it kept the company in business.

The real decision Rolls-Royce faced was whether to branch into aircraft engine development and manufacture in its own right. The engineering quality of its motor cars demonstrated that it was well suited to the task. Yet there was initially general board resistance to the idea. The reasons were not hard to discern. Turning the company over exclusively to manufacture of aircraft engines during hostilities threatened to turn what was a public company into an extension of a government department. The longer-term worry was what would happen once the war was over, at the time generally believed by Christmas. Rolls-Royce would then have lost its loyal traditional customers, the buyers of its motor cars, and might be left without any military aircraft engine orders. Civil aviation at that stage was simply not a feature of travel.

However, the Rolls-Royce board essentially had no choice. By the time its patriotic duty was recognised, Royce was already working on the design of the liquid-cooled V12 aircraft engine that was to carry the name Eagle.

Another company was formed in October 1917 to design and manufacture aircraft engines. From insignificant beginnings, it steadily prospered and then moved into cars and motorcycles. At the end of the century, BMW of Munich bought the car-manufacturing rights to Rolls-Royce.

For many years, the design and manufacture of aircraft, together with the engines to power them, was almost alien territory for Britain, where the War Office and Admiralty seemed oblivious to the likely effects of aerial warfare. Around 1911, the country belatedly began to establish an aircraft industry infrastructure centred on the Royal Aircraft Factory (later Royal Aircraft Establishment) at Farnborough, south-west of London. When war broke out in August 1914, Britain's highly fragmented aircraft industry was still largely rudimentary and heavily reliant on foreign technology.

Royce was to introduce his own original and exacting standards to the aircraft engine business. The design of the Eagle was carried out mainly by Royce at St Margaret's Bay, with drawings and components shuttling between there and Derby. Shortly before Christmas 1915, Rolls-Royce's first aircraft engines, the 250-horsepower Eagles, took to the air at Hendon, north of London, in a giant Handley Page bomber known as 0/100.

The Eagle and its later, more powerful derivatives were a great success. Rolls-Royce manufactured nearly 5,000 of them, and they powered dozens of types of aircraft. Some even went into early battle tanks. The engine continued in service up to the early 1930s. An Eagle-powered Vickers Vimy flown by Alcock and Brown crossed the Atlantic in 1919. Other endurance tests saw Eagles safely power aircraft flying from England to Australia and to what was then Southern

Rhodesia.

Rolls-Royce developed three other series of aircraft engines during this period: the Hawk, a six-cylinder intended for trainer aircraft and airships; the Falcon, a small V12 for fighters; and the Condor, a large V12 for heavy bombers, which appeared just as hostilities ended. The Bristol Fighter, or Brisfit, fitted with a Falcon engine, became Britain's most successful aircraft of its type. Many were made under contract in Bristol by Brazil Straker. The Derby works was extended at government expense to carry out engine repairs. An estimated 60 per cent of all aircraft engines made during the war were by Rolls-Royce, though the company was frequently slow to deliver because of its fastidious development and manufacturing standards, and a general shortage of manpower, materials and machine tools.

The critical question the directors of Rolls-Royce faced was how best to develop the company once hostilities ended.

CHAPTER 4

PICKING UP THE PIECES POST-WAR

T he Great War, which cost 10 million people their lives, was aptly named. Whole generations of young men from both sides, brothers, friends and neighbours, fell in Flanders fields. For the families of the dead, and for the overwhelming majority of survivors, there was a desperate need to return to a normal life after the Armistice was signed in November 1918. But the legacy of war lingered, not least in 1920 when French troops occupied the Ruhr, the heartland of Germany's heavy industry. It was a provocative act that fuelled German nationalism. There were constant worries that the Communist revolution in Russia would find echoes around the world. It was against this background that an Austrian-born former corporal named Adolf Hitler began his rise to power.

However, it was a "good" war for Rolls-Royce, which emerged with an enhanced reputation for engineering excellence. Refinement and reliability became Rolls-Royce hallmarks that passed into popular culture. Chassis production for cars had ceased, but the company survived by continuing to manufacture vehicles for military use while simultaneously diversifying into aircraft engines. The issue for the company to resolve was its role in peace time.

For the future, it would clearly have two disciplines rather than the one when war broke out. The requirement for a steady supply of aircraft engines diminished in the immediate post-war period, but, with a latent, peace-time surge in demand for cars – and everything else – Rolls-Royce decided to increase annual output. This was not just at Nightingale Road. The company embarked on a bold strategy to build cars in one of its most important export markets, the United States. The development, while ultimately not a success, anticipated by at least half a century the wave of foreign-owned car factories that sprang up across the United States.

Royce also quickly began work on the design and development of two all-new models that would initially complement the faithful Silver Ghost – a model whose post-war secondhand values soared in the absence of new products of any kind. However, Royce's newcomers were not available until the first half of the 1920s.

The first model, developed as the Goshawk, was the 20 HP with a six-cylinder 3.1-litre engine. Launched in 1922, it was fondly seen by the public as the "small" Rolls-Royce. The principle behind the Twenty is one that is immediately recognisable today, when sales and marketing methods are more sophisticated. The Twenty filled the roles of the Jaguar X-Type, Mercedes-Benz A-class or BMW 1-series today: a smaller, cheaper model conceived to give its producer wider customer appeal than it had historically enjoyed.

The first Le Mans 24-hours motor race in 1923 was won by Lagache and Leonard in a Chenard et Walcker. One of Britain's new Bentleys won the following year, and on four successive occasions from 1927 to 1931. When Bentley was forced to call in the receivers in 1931, the assets were bought by Rolls-Royce.

However, owners of existing Rolls-Royces were rather dismissive of the Twenty because of its size and modest performance. Even within the company, the Twenty was regarded as something of a poor relation, though subsequent developments – the 20/25 with its 3.7-litre engine of 1929 and the 25/30 with its 4.3-litre of 1936 – improved the model's sales appeal. The final development of the original Twenty was the model known as the Wraith, introduced shortly before the outbreak of the Second World War.

Royce's other new range was the Phantom, a development of the 30/40 powered by a 7.7-litre six-cylinder engine. First launched in 1925, the series of pre-war Phantoms came to epitomise the supreme opulence and style of the era. No self-respecting potentate, prince or personality would settle for anything less. Owners ranged from the Prince of Wales to Charlie Chaplin and land and water speed challenger Malcolm Campbell. The original Phantom was followed by the Phantom II of 1929, and the 7.3-litre V12-powered Phantom III of 1936. When the designers of the 2003 Phantom – the first model introduced under BMW ownership – tried to capture the DNA of Rolls-Royce, they returned again and again to the Phantoms of the 1930s for inspiration. The result is evident in the latest Phantom's height, short front overhang, long bonnet and huge wheels.

Whatever Rolls-Royce's dazzling reputation, the circumstances in which it and other manufacturers found themselves by the early 1920s were difficult. Many of the orders on Rolls-Royce's books dated from before the war. Since then, Rolls-Royce's manufacturing costs had more than doubled. And the immediate post-war spending spree was soon over. Britain's Chancellor of the Exchequer, Winston Churchill, set car tax at £1 per horsepower in 1920, a severe sales handicap for any company making powerful cars. The country also maintained the infamous McKenna duties that added a 33.3 per cent tax to "luxury" imports, that included motor cars. Unemployment in Britain rose steadily after the war. It reached 2 million by 1921, and did not fall below that until the eve of the Second World War. It was accompanied by cuts in public services in order to balance the country's budget. Meanwhile, the strength of sterling accelerated the migration of traditional British industries such as textiles and steel to other countries, adding further to local levels of unemployment.

There were still far too many small, independent car companies, but consolidation began to take place in the 1920s. Ford in 1922 bought Lincoln, a luxury marque founded only five years earlier by former Cadillac engineer Henry Leland. In

Germany, Daimler and Benz merged in 1926. The following year in Britain, Morris bought the failed Wolseley company, and in 1928 the Rootes brothers bought Hillman and Humber.

These economic difficulties helped to foster the unprecedented popularity of small, locally built saloons such as the Austin Seven, Morris Eight, Ford Eight and Standard Eight. Models like these transformed transport for Britain's middle classes in the 1920s and 1930s, and served as a reminder to owners of Rolls-Royces of what Henry Ford described as the democracy of motoring. This curious combination of high unemployment and rising living standards had its origins in the repetitive drudgery of mass production, whose introduction meant that popular car prices practically fell by half in the 1920s.

Mass production was not something that concerned Rolls-Royce. Its craftsmen hand-built the chassis, engines, transmissions, suspension, steering and brakes, in preparation for the craft workers at other companies to mount whatever interior trim and bodywork was specified by the customer.

Several significant new names appeared in the 1920s: the Austin Seven in 1922, the first MGs and Triumphs in 1923, and the first Chryslers in 1924. Earlier, in 1921, a coal merchant's son from Blackpool began making motorcycle sidecars. The man was William Lyons, whose company was to evolve into Jaguar.

Claude Johnson of Rolls-Royce was well aware of the changes taking place in vehicle manufacturing and in society more generally. Despite rising demand, there were still too many competing companies to achieve appropriate economies of scale. But while the industry was too fragmented, proud pioneering egos were at work. Johnson attended a meeting in 1919 with the top managers of Daimler, Wolseley and Vickers to discuss a possible merger. Suspecting an attempted take-over coup by Vickers, Johnson and his colleagues decided to ignore the proposal. Eight years later, the

Wolseley company failed, and in 1931 Daimler bought Lanchester, Britain's oldest motor manufacturer. Vickers would have to wait another six decades before getting its hands on Rolls-Royce.

It was not the first time Johnson had explored the possibility of a merger for Rolls-Royce. He undertook an extended, nine-month tour of the United States after the country entered the war in April 1917 with a view to manufacturing Rolls-Royce Eagle aircraft engines there. The idea came to nothing because the US government was keen to manufacture its own Liberty engines, although Rolls-Royce engineers won praise for their unselfish advice over the development of the unit.

For Johnson, though, the tour presented another possibility: some sort of merger with Pierce-Arrow. The company, founded by Percy Pierce as the Great Arrow Car Company in Buffalo, won the inaugural 1905 Glidden Tour, a landmark, eight-day durability trial that helped to popularise motoring in the United States. The company, renamed Pierce-Arrow in 1908, went on to win the same event over the following four years, cementing its reputation as one of America's premier car makers. Its public image fitted entirely with that of Rolls-Royce.

Johnson's idea was for Pierce-Arrow to make Eagle aircraft engines for the military during the war and later for what he saw as a burgeoning commercial aviation market. Pierce-Arrow would also make Rolls-Royce cars for American customers, while Rolls-Royce would sell Pierce-Arrow's commercial vehicles through its European sales network. The idea came to naught, but Johnson did not give up the idea of making Rolls-Royces in the United States. It was, and remains, the biggest car market in the world, and more of its citizens than any other country's were able to afford Rolls-Royces. Johnson's theory was sound, the execution less so.

Rolls-Royces had been sold in the United States since before the war. Making them in the country would be a very risky undertaking for such a small company, but Rolls-Royce of America Inc. was formed in November 1919 to do just that. Johnson was chairman, but the majority of the directors and most of the capital were

American. The new company's first task was to find a suitable manufacturing location, which it did by selecting a site in Springfield, Massachusetts. The town had a skilled labour force because of its tradition of making machine tools and light armaments. Like the transplants of the late 20th century, it was well removed from Detroit. The Michigan city was by then the centre of the North American vehicle-manufacturing industry, with all that implied in terms of labour confrontation in a rapidly expanding sector.

The idea was to reproduce exactly the quality standards of Derby in Springfield, to such an extent that no customer would be able to tell the difference. What that added up to was *diktat* by Derby. Everything that went into a Springfield Rolls-Royce, whether it involved machine tools, milling standards or steel specifications, was drawn up by Derby. Yet America's engineering standards were not inferior to those in the UK; they were just different. The result was that budgets over-ran because of the need to make cars in America exactly the English way. It was the same kind of engineering arrogance that would rebound on Rolls-Royce many years later in the development of the RB-211 aircraft engine.

Springfield cars were in fact in many ways superior, thanks to the higher standard of many raw materials and locally sourced electrical components. The quality of the coachwork, most of which was produced by Brewster, was also judged by the company to be better than that of many Rolls-Royce suppliers in Britain.

The first Springfield car, completed in 1921, was a 40/50, a series introduced 15 years earlier and whose successors were already under development. Further costs were incurred in modifying the car for the extremes of temperature in the United States, the lower grade of fuel and rougher road conditions. All changes had to be approved by Derby, which added time to the process. Neither did the 40/50 ever get four-wheel brakes, in a period when most of the best locally made cars had them. And those Cadillacs, Lincolns, Packards and others were exceptionally well made, durable cars costing half as much as a Rolls-Royce. An American buyer had seemed prepared to pay handsomely for the social caché of owning a Rolls-Royce because it was made by craftsmen in England. But why would he want to buy an American Rolls-Royce costing twice as much as a Cadillac? And especially one he had to wait several months for while the separate bodywork was constructed and mounted on the chassis?

Sales of these Springfield cars never reached expectations. The factory was designed and equipped for an output of 380 chassis a year, with room for expansion if required. It made fewer than 3,000 during its entire existence. The period following the Wall Street crash of 1929 was hardly a time for conspicuous consumption, even if someone could afford to indulge. The factory limped on, but its assets – renamed Springfield Manufacturing Corp. to avoid damaging the hallowed name – went into liquidation in August 1934.

In a distinguished career at Rolls-Royce, Springfield was Johnson's one big mistake. However, when the closure came, the man widely referred to as the "hyphen" in Rolls-Royce was not there to see it. Johnson died on April 11, 1926 following a bout of pneumonia, exacerbated by years of hard work and worry. He was only 61. Royce lost a friend as well as a colleague. It was Johnson who looked after Royce when the founder was ill, secured him homes on the south coast of England and in France, and removed Royce from the daily grind of Derby. Equally, by doing so, Johnson spared Derby the constant disruptions of Royce's demands.

When the 1920s began, half of all vehicles in the world were Ford Model Ts. When the model finally reached the end of the road in 1927, over 15 million cars had been built in 19 years.

Events in Britain continued to conspire against companies manufacturing luxury items. The country's first ever general strike began less than a month after Johnson died. What started as a strike by coal miners spread throughout the trades union movement. Transport and manufacturing in the country almost ceased, although Britain's middle classes rallied and the army was mobilised to break the strike. Even when the protest petered out after nine days, the miners continued in defiance for several months. As with the events of the early 1980s, militant action proved of no avail to the strikers.

While Rolls-Royce was very busy with the development of its car business, and the diversion of the US operation, it lost some of its importance in the aircraft engine field in the 1920s to competitors like Bristol and Napier. That was to change towards the end of the decade, when Rolls-Royce was prevailed upon to design a high-performance racing engine for an experimental seaplane being developed by the Supermarine company. The development would have repercussions way beyond Britain's determination to win the Schneider Trophy.

The Trophy, first run in 1912, was a speed competition for seaplanes conceived by a Frenchman, Jacques Schneider. As the rules of the competition called for national rather than individual entries, the competition took on huge political importance at a time of rising nationalism in Europe. The regulations also stated that three consecutive wins by any national team would secure the trophy forever. That was what Britain set out to achieve.

The 1927 event was won by a Supermarine S5 designed by R.J. Mitchell and powered by a Napier Lion engine. For the 1929 event, Britain's Air Ministry commissioned another experimental aircraft from Supermarine, the S6. What was needed was a more powerful engine for it. The ministry believed Rolls-Royce was the company for the job. Basil Johnson, who had succeeded his late brother as managing director of Rolls-Royce, did not. He regarded any racing venture as a distraction from the company's main business of making superior, refined motor cars. However, Royce and the Rolls-Royce engineers at Derby were anxious to take up the challenge, and Johnson left the company soon afterwards.

The engine Rolls-Royce came up with was a development of the existing Buzzard V12 equipped with a centrifugal supercharger. Legend has it that Royce used his walking stick to sketch the basic design for his colleagues in the sand on a beach near his West Wittering home. There was little emphasis on durability and ease of servicing. Instead, the R, as the engine became known, was designed to run at full power for relatively short periods. Fitted to the Supermarine S6, and watched by an estimated two million people along the Solent estuary in southern England, Flying Officer H.R. Waghorn won the event with a speed in excess of 328 mph.

Two down, one to go. In the run-up to the crucial third event scheduled for 1931, the political and economic climate in Britain had changed. The ripple effect of the Wall Street crash provoked a financial crisis in Britain, where the government of Labour Prime Minister Ramsay MacDonald did not feel able to underwrite the cost of the air racing venture. Neither did Vickers, the owners of Supermarine. The project was saved only when the wealthy Lady Houston who, in a calculated endorsement of patriotism and a snub for socialism, donated £100,000 towards the cost.

The combination of Mitchell's modified aircraft, designated the Supermarine S6B, and Royce's R engine with an additional 20 per cent horsepower, permanently secured the Schneider Trophy that September. Piloted by Flight Lieutenant G. Stainforth, the S6B also achieved a world record speed of 408 mph. The R engine achieved further fame when it powered Malcolm Campbell's Bluebird and Captain George Eyston's Thunderbolt in various land speed record attempts, as well as water speed record runs by Cambell's Bluebirds and Kaye Don's Miss England. Royce's role in these and other engineering achievements was recognised with a baronetcy in the King's 1930 birthday honours.

As it turned out, the endeavour to win the Schneider Trophy proved to be much more important than the accompanying flag-waving jingoism. Mitchell used the lessons of developing his series of racing seaplanes to create the Supermarine Spitfire. Royce adapted what he learned with the R to design the Merlin aircraft engine. Together, they proved invaluable during the dark days of 1939-45, though neither man would live to see just how vital their contribution was to be.

CHAPTER 5

WHEN ROLLS-ROYCE BOUGHT BENTLEY

The turbulent 1930s were very significant for the Rolls-Royce company in another respect. It was the time when it sneakily acquired Bentley Motors, one of its principal rivals. Having done so, though, the new owner appeared undecided what to do with its prize. Bentley's high-quality products and its well-heeled clientele were too close to those of Rolls-Royce for comfort. It is impossible to escape the conclusion that the primary reason for the purchase was to prevent Bentley from being bought by another rival, rather than Rolls-Royce having a grand strategic vision for the company. What is not in doubt is that Rolls-Royce had no idea what role to assign the eponymous founder of Bentley. The episode turned out to be an unpleasant tale of a talent ignored by a new proprietor blinded by its own achievements.

Walter Owen Bentley was born in 1888, which made him 25 years Henry Royce's junior. But if Bentley's comfortable middle-class background was very different from Royce's peripatetic, hand-to-mouth experience, the two had one thing in common: both served their apprenticeships with the Great Northern Railway, Bentley at Doncaster and Royce at Peterborough a generation earlier. While working in Doncaster, Bentley's early passion for steam power was overtaken by a fascination with the internal combustion engine. He took up motorcycling and, when his apprenticeship was completed, elected to devote his career to the burgeoning car business. Still in his early twenties, W.O., as he was invariably known, went into partnership with his brother, Henry, to sell French-made cars from premises in New Street Mews, just off Baker Street in London.

When war broke out in 1914, Bentley, like all able-bodied countrymen of the time, enlisted. He joined the Royal Navy Air Service, where he became responsible for the design of the BR1 and BR2 air-cooled radial aircraft engines that powered the Sopwith Camel. A firm believer in aluminium pistons, Bentley also managed to convince Rolls-Royce to use them in the aircraft engine it then had under development, the Eagle.

Bentley returned to the same London mews after hostilities, determined to start a car-manufacturing business. The design of the first chassis and engine was undertaken in offices in Conduit Street, and fabrication was completed in New Street Mews, not always to the pleasure of the neighbours. While the prototype of Bentley's first car, a four-cylinder 3-litre, was ready in 1919, a couple of years elapsed before production cars were ready for delivery to customers. It is astonishing that Bentley got that far. His company was constantly under-funded, and even the established companies catering for the motoring needs of the nation's wealthy elite, such as Daimler, Humber, Napier and Sunbeam, found trading conditions very difficult. Rather, the car companies that had the greatest impact on British society at the time were those founded by Herbert Austin and William Morris. The era marked the start of mass motoring, with all that meant in pleasure and pitfalls. For the aristocrats of the car business like Rolls-Royce, the barbarians were at the gate.

Against all the odds, Bentley did succeed in establishing a niche for his high-performance cars among a set of wealthy tear-aways, actors and princes. The company moved out of the mews to a proper factory in Cricklewood, north-west London. Proving the cars in competition was the key. Bentley drivers began winning races at Brooklands, the high-speed circuit in Surrey that boasted "the right crowd and no crowding". Amateur racer and motor dealer John Duff and Frank Clement, the head of Bentley's experimental shop, finished fourth in the first Le Mans 24-hours race in 1923. When they recorded an outright win the following year, it was hard to believe that Bentley Motors was then only five years old.

The legend of the Bentley Boys was born during that time. Young men like Dudley Benjafield, Bertie Kensington Moir, Sammy Davis, Frank Clement, Tim Birkin, Glen Kidston, George Duller, Jack Barclay, Bernard Rubin and Woolf Barnato were gifted amateur sportsmen who competed for the thrill of the chase rather than financial reward. If they drove hard on the race track, they played equally hard in their leisure time. W.O. Bentley later recalled, "The company's activities, particularly in its racing, attracted the public's fancy and added a touch of colour, vicarious glamour and excitement to our drab lives."

Bentley also wrote, "The public liked to imagine them living in expensive Mayfair flats with several mistresses and, of course, several very fast Bentleys, drinking champagne in night clubs, playing the horses and the Stock Exchange, and beating furiously around race tracks at the weekend. Of at least several of them, this was not such an inaccurate picture."

However, money was still tight at Bentley Motors. The problem was solved, at least temporarily, when Barnato agreed in 1926 to take a majority share in the company and became its chairman. As the son of Barney Barnato, who had made a fortune in diamond and gold mining in South Africa with Cecil Rhodes, he could afford to. Woolf Barnato was a gifted all-round athlete who lived life to the full: motor racing, wild parties at his house in Lingfield, Surrey, and summers yachting in the south of France. On one famous occasion in 1930, Barnato decided to pit his $6^1/2$-litre Bentley against the renowned Blue Train from the south of France to London. He arrived $3^3/4$ hours ahead of the train, a remarkable achievement considering the driving conditions of the day.

Once Barnato was in charge, Le Mans became the focal point of Bentley's motor-racing year. Benjafield and Davis won the event with a 3-litre in 1927. Barnato then scored a Le Mans hat-trick, winning with Rubin in a $4^1/2$-litre in 1928, Birkin in a 6.6-litre Speed Six in

1929 and Kidston in another Speed Six the following year. Other Bentleys dominated the top finishing positions throughout the era. Piqued, Ettore Bugatti famously described Bentley's cars as "the fastest lorries in the world". Bentley's five victories (in only eight years) at the French race were not bettered until Jaguar started a series of wins in 1951.

Glorious as the achievements were, Bentley's finances were never sound. Motor racing was an enjoyable and costly diversion from the real challenge of putting Bentley on to a proper commercial footing. The external pressures built up after the ripple effects of the 1929 Wall Street crash reached round the world. Even the wealthy Barnato was not immune. Bentley Motors even approached Rolls-Royce with a view to cost-sharing certain aspects of their businesses. Rolls-Royce declined, understandably wary about the possible scale of any liabilities it might incur if Bentley did fail. Equally, Rolls-Royce directors were conscious of the fact that picking up the pieces in the event of a Bentley collapse would be a cheaper alternative.

Unable to pay its weekly wages bill, Bentley Motors called in the receivers on July 11, 1931. Barnato told the *Financial Times*, "I have personally carried on the company out of my own pocket for the last year, and provided employment directly and indirectly for upwards of 1,500 people." *The Motor* magazine decided the development was not worth reporting at the time. However, its big rival, *The Autocar*, struck an appropriately patriotic (and pedestrian) tone on July 17 when it noted:

> "Every lover of clean sports and a fine sports car will wish Bentley Motors Ltd a speedy issue out of the financial troubles which culminated last week in the appointment of a receiver. The position in which this famous firm finds itself is entirely due to general trade depression that reduces to vanishing point the number of those who can afford to buy very high class and therefore expensive motor cars. It is confidently hoped that Bentleys will soon be on their feet again, and that they will in years to come fly the British flag

in international sporting events with a success no less pronounced than that achieved in the past. Few firms in the
world have acquired so famous a name in so comparatively
short a time."

By the end of the month, the receivers were already in discussion
with D. Napier & Son, of Acton, about a possible take-over of Bentley
assets. Napier was an early motoring pioneer that, like Rolls-Royce,
moved into aircraft engine manufacture. But unlike Rolls-Royce,
Napier dropped out of car manufacture in the mid-1920s to concentrate on aero engines. The idea of a merger appealed to both sides.
Napier would be able to return to the car business and Bentley's
founder would take up aircraft engine design once more. An outline
plan was even drawn up to develop a Napier-Bentley to challenge the
then-new Rolls-Royce Phantom II. While settling all the details
seemed to drag on during that summer and into the autumn, the
belief in the motor business at the time was that the Napier-Bentley
merger was a done deal. It was not.

At the end of November, with the receiver about to implement
the Napier proposal, a counter-offer was received at the last minute
from an organisation calling itself the British Central Equitable
Trust. When the requested sealed bids were opened, the anonymous
trust's offer was found to be a little higher than Napier's. Bentley
Motors had a new owner – but who was it? The answer, according to
W.O. Bentley's autobiography, was provided a few days later when his
wife returned from a party at which she overheard someone called
Arthur Sidgreaves boast that his firm had just bought Bentley. While
she did not know who he was, W.O. did. Sidgreaves was managing
director of Rolls-Royce. The realisation that British Central
Equitable Trust was a front for Rolls-Royce was a tremendous blow
to Bentley, and with good reason as events unfolded.

It transpired that British Central Equitable Trust offered just
over £125,000 for the assets of Bentley, equivalent to around £6.5
million by the start of the 21st century. For nearly two years, it
seemed like a great deal of money for nothing. Output of Bentleys at

Cricklewood was halted. The 1930 8-litre was too close for comfort in the market to Rolls-Royce's own Phantom, and the under-powered 4-litre never appealed greatly to Bentley customers.

As for Bentley himself, Rolls-Royce shamelessly ignored his abilities. He was prevented from taking up an offer to work on aircraft engine development at Napier because Rolls-Royce insisted Bentley was part of the assets it had just acquired. However, Bentley was not assigned to Rolls-Royce's own aero engine operation, or to work on the design of the new generation of cars to bear his name. Instead, he was initially allocated the task of looking after Rolls-Royce's demonstrator models, and was later allowed to carry out road testing. Bentley recalled a meeting shortly after the take-over with the great co-founder of Rolls-Royce, a quarter of a century his senior and recently knighted for his firm's contribution towards the Schneider Trophy wins. Royce, professing not to know that Bentley was an engineer like himself, referred to him as a "commercial man". As the failure of Bentley Motors unkindly demonstrated, "commercial" was the one quality Bentley did not possess. Bentley took the opportunity to remind Royce that he, too, was a former engineering apprentice with the Great Northern Railway.

If the relationship between Royce and Bentley proved unproductive, it was also short. Royce died in April 1933 and Bentley left Rolls-Royce two years later to join Lagonda. There, he designed a V12 engine for a model to rival the Phantom III, and a 2.6-litre six-cylinder subsequently used to power a series of post-war Aston Martins after David Brown bought the company. W.O. Bentley died in 1971.

The first Derby Bentley was introduced in 1933. It had nothing in common with any model that preceded it, except the name. It was perhaps a precursor of the development that took place at Bentley after Volkswagen bought the company at the end of the century. The first Derby Bentley used the chassis of an abandoned Rolls-Royce project, the Peregrine, a Rolls-Royce engine with a higher performance, and was developed wholly by Rolls-Royce. While the $3^1/2$ (actual engine displacement was 3.7 litres) and later $4^1/4$, which were successfully promoted as "silent sports cars", were much admired, they were the Rolls-Royce engineering department's idea of what Bentleys should be, not W.O. Bentley's.

Derby made a respectable total of just over 2,400 Bentleys in the seven years up to 1939. During that period, Rolls-Royce embarked on a project to develop its so-called rationalised range, conceived to eliminate the engineering and manufacturing diversity between its models. In other words, what Rolls-Royce did then was just what a modern car maker does today by having several models make use of the same basic platform and powertrain.

The Bentley Mk V of 1939, the first model to emerge from Rolls-Royce's rationalised range, was also the first Bentley to feature independent front suspension. It used a $4^1/_4$ litre six-cylinder engine and featured a riveted frame chassis with cruciform centre bracing. An experimental version was tested with a radically different and streamlined body designed by Georges Paulin. It was known as the Corniche – a model name that remained a matter of dispute long after Volkswagen bought Bentley and BMW acquired the rights to Rolls-Royce – and was effectively the forerunner of the post-war Continental R. However, Europe and the world were about to change. Only 11 Bentley Mk Vs were completed before Prime Minister Neville Chamberlain told the House of Commons at noon on September 3, 1939, "This country is now at war with Germany."

CHAPTER 6

THE END OF AN ERA

The long-term future of Rolls-Royce was determined by two significant developments in the 1930s. First was the death of the co-founder, an event that prompted the company to undertake a thorough internal review of the way it was organised. Close inspection revealed the review was sorely needed. Externally, it was inevitable that the rising tide of nationalism in Germany, Italy and Japan would at some stage have a profound effect on the rest of the world. The implications for Rolls-Royce, which was a major supplier of aircraft and vehicle engines to Britain's military establishment, completely changed the balance of its business. It was the decade when Rolls-Royce's work on aircraft engines overtook that of the car business for good.

Sir Henry Royce died at his home in West Wittering on April 22, 1933, nearly four weeks after his 70th birthday. He was a remarkable man, a hard-working engineering visionary who was unprepared to compromise on quality. The Royce philosophy was epitomised by one of his many sayings: "Whatever is rightly done, however humble, is noble". Overcoming the difficulties of his early circumstances, Royce was still in his early forties when he created the Silver Ghost that would come to be widely acknowledged as "the best car in the world". The design of the final car for which he was wholly responsible, the V12-engined Phantom III of 1936, symbolised the man and the company. The Phantom III represented a blind pursuit of engineering perfection. In reality, it was a vainglorious triumph of ambition over practicality and commercial sense.

Health permitting, Royce worked long hours from his design offices in West Wittering and Le Canadel, setting the engineering tone for all Rolls-Royce vehicles and aircraft engines. The co-founder's word on engineering matters was law within Rolls-Royce. For Royce, getting the design of a piece of equipment right was more important than the cost or timescale involved in its manufacture. Royce's remote existence was a classic example of the person who lived in an ivory tower. Removed from the blunt end of manufacturing at Derby, and from the sharp end of commerce at Conduit Street, where the late Claude Johnson's presence was deeply missed, Royce did not understand what was happening in the world beyond the cloisters of his protected existence. In cars at least, Rolls-Royce no longer had the quality and refinement edges it believed it had, as a coruscating internal memo after Royce's death revealed.

Rolls-Royce's unfortunate manufacturing adventure in the United States exposed some of its personnel to the high quality and low costs achieved by that country's car makers. Top American marques such as Cadillac, Duesenberg, Lincoln, Marmon and Packard achieved quality levels as good as Rolls-Royce, but with far greater reliability and much lower prices. Many were technically advanced as well. Duesenberg's Model J of 1928, for example, had a twin overhead camshaft straight-eight engine that used four valves per cylinder and made extensive use of aluminium in its construction. Packard, Lincoln and Pierce-Arrow boasted V12s. Not to be outdone, Cadillac brought out a V16 in the mid-1930s.

Because the American car market was so large, local producers could justify greater automation in their factories. Higher sales provided vehicle makers with greater purchasing power, which consequently lowered the cost of bought-in supplies. This aspect of the business meant much less to Rolls-Royce, where everything from carburettors to shock absorbers, from radiators to steering gear, were designed, perfected and fabricated in-house. For Rolls-Royce, it was irrelevant that component suppliers could sell it the same things at a sixth of the price; no one could do the job better than the co-founder and his team of engineers and designers. The philosophy was an engineering dead end. Tellingly, it was one which Rolls-Royce reversed as soon as was decently possible after Royce's death.

Elsewhere in Europe, superlative cars by Bugatti, Delage, Hispano-Suiza, Horch, Isotta-Fraschini and Mercedes-Benz were worthy alternatives to Rolls-Royce. However the impact on Rolls-Royce was minimal, protected as it and other British car makers were by the McKenna duty, which added one-third to import prices. The warning signs were there, however. The much-admired Phantom, a series that inspired BMW's Rolls-Royce designers seven decades later, was not a great sales success. The average annual sales of the original Phantom, including those manufactured in Springfield, were just over 490. The annual average for the Series II was barely more than 220. When the Series III appeared, the average dipped to 180 a year. In other words, as the Phantoms were gradually perfected, and during a period when demand for cars in general was on the increase, their appeal to customers steadily declined. Worse, the Phantoms had no more than a handful of components in common with other models in the Rolls-Royce and Bentley ranges.

Phantom was an Olympian technical achievement lacking in commercial logic. Like the Concorde supersonic airliner project of the late 20th century, it was visually beautiful, but unsaleable, impractical and unaffordable. It was made possible only by the co-founder's unchallenged position within the company, and the financial distortions flowing from Rolls-Royce's burgeoning aero engine work. While the government – in other words, taxpayers – funded the much-needed re-armament programme, what did it matter that the Phantom lost money? In the post-war period, Rolls-Royce's managing director vowed never to return to the "Phantom III mentality".

Indeed most of the rest of the country's car makers flourished during that period, particularly those making popular models, whose prices actually went down. In five years in the early 1930s, the price of a Ford Model Y was gradually cut by over 15 per cent to £100. Austin and Morris could only follow. By contrast, a Phantom

III chassis (the bodywork was extra, of course) was priced at nearly £1,900. Meanwhile, around that time a good-quality Rover saloon cost £450, while a handsome Queen Anne house set in nine acres of Oxfordshire could be bought for £3,400. Britain's car makers thrived because they enjoyed a protected domestic market and the vast sales potential offered by the British Empire. The British car industry overtook that of France in the mid-1930s to rank second in the world only to that of the United States. Tellingly, though, while American makers produced 15 times more cars a year than those in Britain, they did so with a workforce that overall was only twice the size. While postponed by the 1939-45 conflict, the lack of competitiveness and productivity would eventually come to haunt all car makers in Britain, including Rolls-Royce.

The death of Royce provided Rolls-Royce with the opportunity to re-organise the company. Royce's studios in Sussex and the south of France were closed. A single design and engineering department responsible for cars and aircraft engines was created at Nightingale Road, Derby. Arthur Sidgreaves was the firm's managing director, and his general manager at Derby was Arthur Wormald, a man in failing health who had been with Rolls-Royce since its formation. When Wormald died in 1936, Sidgreaves assigned the general manager's job to Ernest Hives, at the time head of the company's experimental department. It proved a turning point for Rolls-Royce at a critical moment in the company's history, and that of the country.

Hives began his career as a 12-year-old apprentice in a bicycle shop in Reading. Following a chance encounter, he became personal chauffeur to Charles Rolls and then worked for C.S. Rolls & Co. and H.R. Owen, another car dealer. He joined Napier, one of Rolls-Royce's great rivals, where the attraction of racing its cars at Brooklands was irresistible. Hives was still only 22 when he joined Rolls-Royce in 1908. He later recalled that it was raining so hard on the day he arrived at Derby station, and the town looked so drab, that he flipped a coin to decide whether or not to stay.

As a Rolls-Royce tester, Hives was involved in the company's early reliability trials. By the time he was 30, though, he was head of

Rolls-Royce's experimental department, which meant that, in addition to the established car business, Hives was in at the start of its pioneering work on aircraft engines. Much of that endeavour in the late 1920s revolved around the R racing engine that powered the Schneider Trophy-winning Supermarines. When Hives was appointed general manager in 1936, work had only recently begun on the critical engine that was developed as a result of the R experience, the famous Merlin. As the country re-armed, the Royal Air Force was desperate for early Merlin deliveries for its Fairey Battle bomber and Hawker Hurricane and Supermarine Spitfire fighters. In his new position, Hives was pivotal to the completion of the Merlin development programme and for its manufacture at a time of critical national need.

Hives was at the peak of his career in 1936. He was 50 years old and had spent most of his working life in charge of advanced engineering at Rolls-Royce. While he knew intimately the way Rolls-Royce operated, he was also familiar enough with the products of his company's competitors in the United States and other parts of Europe to recognise the flaws in Derby's structure. As the new general manager, he had the energy and ambition to do something about the weaknesses. What Hives told his fellow directors would have an echo more than 60 years later when Ferdinand Piëch became chairman of Volkswagen: the group was like a duck grown too fat to fly.

This period of Rolls-Royce history is best recorded in Alec Harvey-Bailey's book written for the Rolls-Royce Heritage Trust, *Hives, the Quiet Tiger*. "There is no outstanding merit in our cars to make a customer desire to possess one," Hives succinctly told the Rolls-Royce board of directors, which he had just joined. Hives went on to outline the engineering issues faced by the company in the vehicle and aero engine sectors. Testing other companies' cars embarrassingly revealed that a number of them were equal to what was said to be "the best car in the world". The fact that Rolls-Royce was selling a lot of cars at the time was because of a protected home market and a patriotic desire to support local producers. He cited numerous deficiencies in the aircraft engine side, which he said was wholly dependent on work commissioned by the country's military during the accelerating re-armament period. What that effectively meant was that the British taxpayer indirectly underwrote the basis of Rolls-Royce's car business. Uniquely among aero engine manufacturers, Rolls-Royce had no orders from civil airlines, which scrutinised purchase prices and operating costs more critically than the military.

Hives said the remote way in which the company operated when the all-powerful Henry Royce was alive removed the designers and engineers from manufacturing responsibility and slowed decision-making. While the bases in Sussex and the south of France were by then gone, the culture they created was still in place. Hives was also critical of the absence of the manufacturing side at the monthly business reviews, of the lack of any long-term planning, of the paucity of investment that meant half the machinery at Derby was over 20 years old, and of the lavish budget of the experimental department that he formerly ran. The emphasis in the factory centred on brawn and craftsmanship, not brain, he said. Except in scale, the atmosphere of the place had changed very little since it was opened in 1908.

Hives' report amounted to a stunning indictment of a company that had atrophied. With the full support of the board, he began to take steps to solve Rolls-Royce's problems. The chassis and aero engine businesses were separated in all disciplines in July 1937, including design, engineering, testing and manufacture. Quality problems with the Bentley $4^1/4$ and Phantom III were addressed, but the main development was to start work on what was referred to as a "rationalised range" of new chassis and engines. It was needed because the company at the time produced three models, the 25/30, Phantom and Bentley, which had virtually nothing in common.

The chassis division under Robert Harvey-Bailey and William (Roy) Robotham, the chief engineer, was responsible for the rationalised range. Borrowing from principles seen in the American car industry, the range they conceived would be able to accommodate three different engines (four, six and eight cylinders, but with numerous common components) across a standard chassis capable of being made with various wheelbase lengths. There would be a standardisation of most body styles, which would be made easier by Rolls-Royce's 1938 purchase of the Park Ward coachbuilding firm.

Some of the lessons were applied to the 1938 Rolls-Royce Wraith, but the first real model to emerge from the rationalised range was the 1939 Bentley Mk V. It included a high performance version known as the Corniche, which was scheduled to go on sale in 1940. Political events overtook the programme, of course. Eleven Mk Vs were completed by the time war was declared. While car-building went into abeyance, Rolls-Royce and Bentley would at least have modern building blocks to re-start once peace was restored.

CHAPTER 7

ROLLS-ROYCE GOES TO WAR

R olls-Royce aircraft engine production, whose value overtook that of the famous luxury cars in 1935, dominated the company during the Second World War, and after. No vehicles were produced in the seven years following the start of the war, and when output did resume, it was in a new location. The Rolls-Royce chassis division's days at Derby were done. Indeed, as part of the dispersal of people and facilities in case of air raids, the car side's experimental section was relocated a few miles away in an unsavoury former foundry at Clan, near Belper. Everything car-related went into safe storage, including blueprints of the new models. They were never to return to Derby, because the car business was given a new home in Crewe when the war was over.

Britain continued to produce handfuls of other cars throughout the war, but it was not a priority. Fewer than 2,000 were made in 1940, compared with 305,000 in the year war broke out. Instead, the country's vehicle industry was almost wholly turned over to the war effort. Factories that only a few years earlier made popular family saloons found themselves producing army lorries, engines, guns, shells, armoured cars, tanks, bombers and fighters.

The car companies also produced this equipment in a series of brand new factories scattered across the country. Those were the so-called shadow factories, built, equipped and funded by the Air Ministry in a crash programme beginning in the spring of 1936. The vehicle makers' role, made more difficult because of mobilisation and often inadequate local housing, was to run these factories and to find and train the staff to operate them. After the war, the factories were transferred to the car companies for more peaceful production. Examples still in operation in the early 21st century were Longbridge (then Austin and now the home of MG Rover), Castle Bromwich (now a Jaguar factory), Solihull (Land Rover), Ryton (a Peugeot site that once belonged to the Rootes group) and Southampton (where Ford makes vans).

Rolls-Royce, whose aircraft engines were desperately needed by the Royal Air Force, accepted responsibility for two more factories. General manager Ernest Hives wanted to expand the Derby site to produce the engines, but the scale of the expected requirement persuaded him to take on shadow factories. Sites at Shrewsbury, Worcester, Stafford and Burton-on-Trent were considered, but in the end Rolls-Royce went to factories being built on Merrill's Farm, Crewe, and at Hillington, near Glasgow. Rolls-Royce employment increased four-fold to over 55,000 people in the four years to 1943. Derby, Crewe and Hillington made thousands of Merlins. Others were made by Ford at Trafford Park, Manchester, and in the United States by Packard for the US Army Air Force's long range P-51 Mustang fighter.

The Merlin, which began as a private initiative by the Rolls-Royce company as the PV12, is an emotional icon to everyone in Britain interested in history. It was used to power the Hurricanes and Spitfires that became Britain's last line of defence in the summer of 1940. Other Merlins went into the Lancaster and Halifax bombers and the versatile Mosquito, and were used after the war in Canadair DC4 and BOAC Tudor and Argonaut airliners. However, as technically good as the Merlin was, Rolls-Royce proved unable to meet its delivery commitments to the Air Ministry until early 1938, roughly 15 months behind the original schedule, according to the historian Corelli Barnett in his book, *The Audit of War*. Combined with the over-optimistic delivery promises by the manufacturers of the Hurricane and Spitfire fighters, these delays were at the heart of the country's lack of readiness for war. Rolls-Royce's other main aircraft engine of the period was the Griffon, which had a displacement one-third greater than that of the Merlin and more direct design links to the Schneider Trophy-winning R engine. The Griffon was used in later versions of the Spitfire and Seafire and in the post-war Shackleton maritime reconnaissance aircraft. Meanwhile, the experimental department located in Clan was kept busy on tank projects. Its role was to develop a suitable engine using the Merlin as a basis. The resulting Meteor, a Merlin without a supercharger, was used in a series of British battle tanks, including the Cromwell, Comet, Crusader and Centurion. As it turned out, the Meteor proved an unexpected, and highly beneficial, project that changed the future for Rolls-Royce.

Frank Whittle, an RAF officer, published his revolutionary concept on jet propulsion in 1928. Predictably, jet theories were largely ignored by the Air Ministry and the RAF, though not by German aircraft manufacturer Heinkel, whose He 178 became the first jet-powered aircraft to fly, a week before Britain declared war on Germany. Against considerable odds, Whittle's own experimental jet flew for the first time in May 1941 in the Gloster E28/39. The flight was judged a great success, and the Air Ministry, which sponsored the Gloster Whittle project, ordered production versions.

The Rover car company, which built Whittle's prototype, was commissioned to build the production versions once development was finished. However, there were numerous technical delays, as well as acrimony between Whittle and Maurice Wilks, the technical director of Rover. When Hives offered to take over Rover's jet engine commitment in exchange for Rolls-Royce's Meteor tank engine business, Wilks was only too happy to agree. It was the start of a new direction for Rolls-Royce.

CHAPTER 8

A TIME OF CLOUDS
AND SHADOWS

The early turbojet engine experiments propelled Rolls-Royce into a new era after the war. In military and civil aviation, the age of the internal combustion engine gave way to gas turbine engines, which, despite the newness of the technology, were more powerful, more reliable, more efficient, simpler and quieter. Rolls-Royce was responsible for a series of very successful new aircraft engines, starting with the turboprop Dart (a jet that drove propellers) used in the Vickers Viscount airliner and the pure jet Avon. The Avon was installed in a wide variety of front line RAF aircraft of the time, including the Hawker Hunter and Supermarine Swift fighters, the English Electric Canberra bomber and Lightning interceptor and the Vickers Valiant V-bomber. Others were used by Fairey for the experimental FD2 that established a new world speed record of nearly 1,200 mph, and by de Havilland for its ground-breaking Comet airliner. Other successful gas turbines such as the Conway and Spey followed.

The post-war period was one of enormous consolidation in Britain's aircraft industry, as companies, and the government of the day, tried to find the scale to compete with their American rivals. In the aircraft engine arena, Bristol bought Armstrong-Siddeley in 1959, and de Havilland two years later. When Rolls-Royce then took over Bristol in 1966, the country had one enormous and diverse aero engine maker with a chance to compete globally with General Electric and Pratt & Whitney of the United States.

That was the big picture as far as Rolls-Royce was concerned. Its future was wholly dictated by its performance in the aircraft engine sector. The business of producing handfuls of supreme luxury motor cars each year became almost an irrelevance. The two sides of the business certainly had nothing in common since the arrival of gas turbine technology. Jet power was sporadically tried by various car makers (not Rolls-Royce) in experimental models, but none was able to match the performance, costs and practicality of the internal combustion engine. So, by the 1960s, the vast and sprawling aircraft engine operation of Rolls-Royce had nothing in common with the tiny car division. Their technologies, their development times, their costs and their customers were totally different.

With hindsight, it is now possible to discern the vulnerability of the Rolls-Royce car division. The company was at the forefront of aircraft engine technology, but was in a time warp where cars were concerned. And yet, consolidation was also taking place in the motor industry. The merger of Austin and the Nuffield Organisation (Morris, MG, Riley and Wolseley) to form BMC came in 1952. At the time, it was the largest car maker in the world outside the United States. In the mid-1960s, BMC took over Jaguar and Daimler, and Standard-Triumph bought Rover and Land Rover. All of them then came together in 1968 to form the ultimately doomed British Leyland. Chrysler gradually bought Simca's French and Spanish operations and those of Britain's Rootes group (Hillman, Humber, Singer and Sunbeam) in the 1960s. Mercedes-Benz, having failed to secure ownership of BMW in 1959, tried to buy Audi a decade later, only to lose out to Volkswagen. In an equally important move, Ford began in 1967 to create a single entity for its competing European operations.

None of those developments had anything directly to do with Rolls-Royce at the time. Later it did, because each merger had the effect of further reducing the significance of Rolls-Royce. It was also the period when Volkswagen and BMW built the foundations of great companies that by the end of the century were powerful enough to buy Bentley and Rolls-Royce. So, while consolidation brought sweeping changes to the aero engine business and the motor industry, the insular little car division of Rolls-Royce carried on as if the world stood still. Worthy pre-war competitors like Bugatti, Duesenberg, Hispano-Suiza, Horch, Isotta-Fraschini and Packard were gone, and Cadillac, Daimler and Lincoln were shadows of their former existences. While Mercedes-Benz was able to remind the world of its potential by producing the enormous and complex 600, Rolls-Royce had the premium luxury market largely to itself in the decades after the war.

Some indication of Rolls-Royce's special position in the motoring firmament can be judged by its policy on the Phantom IV. The origins of the model lie in a modified Silver Wraith chassis and the eight-cylinder version of the rationalised engine range. A few prototypes were built, but, mindful of the history of earlier Phantoms and the post-war mood of austerity, the company was reluctant to offer the new model for sale. It relented only under pressure from the Duke of Edinburgh, the young husband of Britain's future queen.

The first Phantom IV, a giant state limousine with bodywork by H.J. Mulliner, was presented to Princess Elizabeth and the duke in 1950. The underlying motivation for Rolls-Royce was prestige rather than financial reward, because the appearance of the Phantom IV in the Royal Mews spelled the end of the British royal family's traditional preference for Daimlers on state occasions. Half a century later, Rolls-Royce lost the royal warrant to its former stablemate, Bentley.

However, the interesting perspective, barely believable in the early 21st century, was the shameless Rolls-Royce snobbery surrounding the Phantom IV. It dictated that under no circumstances was the model to be supplied to anyone who was not a member of a royal family or a head of state. A further 17 were supplied over the following six years. The implications of the policy were that any dubious duke, as long as he was royal, a dictator such as Spain's General Franco, or a puppet president in Persia was an acceptable owner of a Phantom IV, but successful entrepreneurs and philanthropists were not. They would have to wait until the Phantom V of 1959, or the Phantom VI of 1968, which continued in tiny volume production until 1992. The Mk IV episode was another indicator of just how removed Rolls-Royce was from the truth of Henry Ford's observation about the democratising effect of motoring, even in the 1950s.

The car side of Rolls-Royce was re-created after the war as the car division, rather than the pre-war chassis division. It was headed by "Doc" Llewellyn-Smith, who oversaw the resumption of car output in the new Crewe factory. The first car produced there was a Bentley Mk VI in October 1946. The company correctly judged that Bentley had an egalitarian face more in tune with the times than the blatantly elitist Rolls-Royce. Investment in Rolls-Royce would have to wait until austerity had eased.

The Labour Party's landslide general election victory of July 1945 was achieved on the back of promises to create a national health service, a welfare state system, and a huge programme of low-cost house-building by local authorities. Labour also embarked on a programme of nationalisation of transport, coal mining and steel production. The fact that it could not afford any of this because of wartime debts, enormous reconstruction costs, and the country's continuing defence commitments around the globe was neither here nor there. Later, there was bread rationing, which had not been imposed during the war, and power shortages during the severe winter of 1947. These were further reminders of the difficulties of living in Britain, and doing business there, in the years after the war.

The quality, and quantity, of steel available to the motor industry during that period was very poor. This posed particular problems for Crewe, where it was determined that future models in the core rationalised range would have standard steel bodies rather than bodies built to order by specialist coachbuilders. The decision was largely forced on Rolls-Royce by the decline of the country's coachbuilding sector. The process started before the war, and accelerated afterwards due to shortages of skills and materials. Most of the country's famous old coachbuilders went out of business, though Rolls-Royce added H.J. Mulliner in 1959 to the Park Ward business it bought a couple of decades earlier.

Instead, Rolls-Royce turned to the Pressed Steel Company for the standard steel bodies of the post-war cars. They were fabricated in Oxford and transported to Crewe, where they were mounted on chassis and finished by hand. The first Silver Dawn, the Rolls-Royce equivalent of the Mk VI, appeared at the end of 1948. The cars were destined for export for the following five years as part of a government initiative to earn desperately needed foreign currency. They went mainly to the United States, where the Rolls-Royce name was reasonably well established and Bentley was virtually unknown. Some indication of Rolls-Royce's sales priorities during that period can be drawn from production numbers for the virtually identical models. The company made over 7,700 Mk VIs (including later R-series) during the nine years to 1955, compared with one-tenth of that number of Silver Dawns from 1949 to 1955.

When the experimental department finally made the move from Clan to Crewe in 1951, it was with a new engineering chief, Harry Grylls, and a new designer, John Blatchley. Both made lasting marks on the car division, because they were responsible respectively for the engineering and design of the 1955 Silver Cloud and the Silver Shadow that replaced it a decade later. More than any others, they shaped the appeal of Rolls-Royce once the immediate after-effects of the war were overcome.

The Silver Cloud and its Bentley S-series twin were widely admired at the time, a reason why they and the pre-war Phantoms were the models most studied by designers undertaking research for the 2003 Phantom. The Silver Cloud defined the age in terms of understated elegance, proportion and line. The model continued the practice established for the Mk VI and Silver Dawn by using a separate chassis mounted with a standard steel body from Pressed Steel. In the new model, though, the chassis was a much stiffer, box-section type. The engine was the company's familiar 4.9-litre straight-six for the first four years of the models' life, after which they received a 6.2-litre V8 featuring a cylinder block and heads made of light aluminium alloy.

Another innovation (for Rolls-Royce at least) was the four-speed automatic transmission. This Hydramatic unit was initially bought as a built-up unit from General Motors, but Rolls-Royce subsequently made the units under licence. Half a century later, a decision to build transmissions in-house would be regarded as an unaffordable luxury for a model whose total output would not exceed 16,000 cars. It was, of course, a legacy of the old Rolls-Royce mindset that insisted no one else could be trusted to do a job so well.

The Silver Cloud was the model that returned Rolls-Royce to marque dominance within the company. The Bentley S-series was initially the more popular, but when production of the series ended, Bentleys accounted for only 47 per cent of them. That compared with around 80 per cent for the two models' predecessors, and only 7 per cent for their successors. The end of the S-series also marked a four-decade suspension of the much-admired Continental name-plate. Initially sold on the R chassis, the fastback saloon was continued on the S-series chassis with a very similar design.

The Silver Shadow and T-series that replaced the Silver Cloud/S-series in 1965 proved a revolution for the car division. It was visually and technically unlike anything previously produced by the company. The more conventional three-box shape, once more the work of Blatchley, finally meant goodbye to the general shape that was associated with Rolls-Royce before and after the war. The Silver Shadow at last looked like a product of the second half of the 20th century. In the modern manner, it was considerably smaller than previous Rolls-Royces, although the space for passengers and their luggage was greater.

While the rest of the international motor industry abandoned the Rolls-Royce method of construction requiring separate chassis and body units, the Silver Shadow was the company's first model to use unitary construction. Pressed Steel was the supplier once more. The model was also the first Rolls-Royce to acquire disc brakes rather than drums, even if the rest of the motor industry had moved to discs long before. Its front and rear suspension, which was mounted on sub-frames, was independent for the first time, though Jaguar had already used all-independent suspension with its Mk X of 1961. The Silver Shadow had a complex hydraulic system that automatically adjusted the ride height according to the vehicle's load and speed. Installing the system required the company to take out certain licences from Citroën, whose DS model of 1955 pioneered this type of self-levelling suspension.

In the best Rolls-Royce traditions, then, none of the various technical aspects of the Silver Shadow was new. Like Henry Royce before them, Grylls and his team took what existed and set about improving it. The Silver Shadow represented a remarkable achievement for a small firm, an achievement that was well rewarded in the market place. The Silver Shadow caught the public imagination at a time of steadily increasing prosperity, reflected a few years earlier by Prime Minister Harold Macmillan when he told an audience: "Most of our people never had it so good". The observation was underlined by the number of cars made and sold in Britain. Annual car production exceeded 1 million for the first time in 1958, and topped 1.5 million five years later. Car registrations in Britain first reached 1 million in 1963, aided by easier credit and the arrival of two important economy models, the BMC Mini and the Ford Anglia. Generally increasing wealth in Britain, and in the rest of the world, meant the Silver Shadow easily became the most popular Rolls-Royce of the modern era. It achieved sales of over 32,000 in its 15-year life cycle, or double the number of Silver Clouds/S-series sold during the 10 years of their existence.

The success of the Silver Shadow put the Rolls-Royce car division in its strongest position in years. Which was just as well, because the parent company had by then got itself into all sorts of trouble in the aero engine business.

CHAPTER 9

DOWN, BUT NOT OUT

Tom Purves recalls very well the moment he learned that his world-famous employer had collapsed. As the Rolls-Royce car division's young sales representative in the north of England and Scotland, he was driving from Edinburgh to Glasgow, on his way to visit A & D Fraser, the company's dealer in the city. He knew the dealership had also just delivered a large consignment of Morris vans to another division of Rolls-Royce, and at that stage had not been paid for them. Under the dramatic new circumstances, Fraser was concerned about whether it was ever going to get its money.

Purves contacted his office for guidance. "I was told to continue with the planned meeting, but to park my car round the corner and under no circumstances to hand over the keys," he recalled over three decades later. By that time, Purves was president of BMW of North America, and therefore ultimately responsible for selling the group's new generation Phantom in the world's largest car market for luxury cars. "We understood the company was in serious problems, but we didn't understand the magnitude of them," Purves added.

On February 4, 1971, Rolls-Royce became Britain's largest postwar bankruptcy. The country's 14th largest group, and Europe's largest aero engine manufacturer, Rolls-Royce employed 84,000 people, most of whom were engaged in aero engine work. It was a humiliation for a proud company, and for a country that regarded Rolls-Royce as solid as the Bank of England. People who had for decades been reminded almost daily of the primacy of Rolls-Royce aero engines (in Spitfires, Hawker Hunters, Vickers Viscounts) and motor cars (Queen Elizabeth II in her state limousine) were presented with a different reality. The ebullience of the swinging sixties ended with a jolt. If Rolls-Royce was so seriously flawed, was, by implication, the country?

The cause of the collapse had nothing to do with the car business. It had everything to do with the development of the giant RB-211 turbofan engine for a new generation of wide-bodied airliners. Quite simply, Rolls-Royce had failed to deliver on its promises. It had set hopelessly ambitious technology and price targets, an unrealistic timetable for the engine's development, and budgets that over-ran within months. Rolls-Royce's creditors, and taxpayers in the UK, paid the price.

The episode illustrated once more the dangers of mono-culture corporations. In Rolls-Royce's case, it was the supremacy of engineering and technology. The engineers had acquired unchallenged pre-eminence because of Rolls-Royce's tremendous historical achievements. But the decision-makers often had only a tenuous grasp of financial and commercial reality. The engineers believed that all problems could be overcome by ingenuity and long working hours, simply because they said so.

Frederick Corfield, the aviation minister, told the House of Commons on the day of the collapse: "It's clear with the benefit of hindsight that the financial control exercised by this company has been of a very mediocre order for a long time." By that time, though, the two principal driving forces behind the RB-211 project – engineers both – had left Rolls-Royce: Sir Denning Pearson, the chief executive, and Sir David Huddie, managing director of the aero engine division. The official government report into the collapse, published in August 1973 by R.A. McCrindle, QC, and P. Godfrey, FCA, said Rolls-Royce had made a "rash commitment" to develop the RB-211. The authors came to the conclusion: "They (Pearson and Huddie) failed to discharge the responsibilities of stewardship which rest upon directors of public companies."

However, while the business strategy that led to the collapse was a risk, it seemed worth taking at the time. Rolls-Royce wanted to get into the emerging "big jet" market, and it wanted to expand in North America. Airlines in the United States in the mid-1960s saw an emerging demand for three-engined, wide-bodied jets smaller then the new four-engined Boeing 747 but larger than the existing narrow-bodied airliners of Boeing and Douglas. Douglas proposed the DC-10, and Lockheed, anxious to re-enter the airliner market, countered with the L-1011, a model that later acquired the TriStar name. Both were designed to offer lower seatmile costs than existing aircraft.

To power them, though, they needed huge, all-new engines. General Electric and Pratt & Whitney, American's main aero engine manufacturers, put forward the CF6 and JT-9D respectively. More controversially, because it would mean an American airframe manufacturer buying engines sourced in the United Kingdom, with all that meant in terms of employment and trade balances, Rolls-Royce began vigorously promoting its RB-211 concept.

The RB-211 was a very advanced three-shaft turbofan that used a composite material known as Hyfil for its giant, two-metre fan blades. Rolls-Royce promised the engine would produce about twice as much thrust as anything it had built up to that point. In order to secure a contract with an airframe maker, it guaranteed the unit price as well as certain noise and economy definitions. And it promised deliveries of production-ready engines in four years.

As it turned out, it was several promises too far. But it was one Lockheed found impossible to resist. When Lockheed awarded the contract to Rolls-Royce in March 1968, it became Britain's largest ever export order. Rolls-Royce was the toast of the City and Whitehall. All it had to do was deliver. The engine maker knew it would have to commit half its workforce to the project if the L-1011 was to launch on schedule in 1972. Wisely, as it turned out for the longer-term success of the RB-211, Lockheed insisted on a parallel programme by which the Hyfil blades could be replaced by ones made of titanium.

Publicly, the Lockheed order was a gung-ho triumph for British engineering. Internally, though, there were deep reservations about being able to meet the conditions of the contract. The theory behind using a carbon fibre composite for the fan blades was sound, though in practical applications it proved the engine's handicap. Hyfil would mean less weight, which aided fuel economy, and higher operating temperatures, which increased the thrust. But the blades proved too fragile in flight testing, particularly if subjected to bird strikes. Trying to solve the problems added weeks, then months, to the project, which eventually slipped more than a year behind schedule. The complications also pushed up the development cost, from an estimated £65 million when the project was conceived to over £200 million by the time the over-runs became a national issue. The inspectors' subsequent official investigation also revealed that actual production costs would be above the delivery prices Rolls-Royce was locked into.

The share price of Rolls-Royce went into freefall as the scale of the problems became more widely understood. There was a very real danger, later realised, that one of the country's major defence contractors would go bust. The Royal Air Force was almost wholly reliant on Rolls-Royce. The Royal Navy's Buccaneers and Phantoms used Rolls-Royce engines. So did the Army's scout cars, personnel carriers and main battle tanks. Even the Olympus engines in Concorde, the high-profile Anglo-French supersonic airliner project, were down to Rolls-Royce following its 1966 take-over of Bristol-Siddeley.

Rolls-Royce was already over its borrowing limits, and the RB-211 was still sucking huge sums out of the company. The Conservative government of Edward Heath, newly elected on a promise of returning state assets to private ownership, reluctantly bailed out Rolls-Royce with nearly £90 million in November 1970. It did not solve the problem: Rolls-Royce was technically insolvent. After the management finally admitted defeat in early February 1971, *The Economist* likened the company to "a tired horse lying down and dying between the shafts". The share price was 7 shillings and 6 pence (37.5 pence) when it was finally suspended, or about one-seventh of the level two years earlier.

E. Rupert Nicholson, of Peat, Marwick, Mitchell & Co., was appointed the official receiver of what became Rolls-Royce (1971) Ltd. The company's aero engine assets were later transferred to government ownership, which was ironic in view of Prime Minister Heath's belief that states should not own businesses. It was not until 18 years later, when Margaret Thatcher was prime minister, that Rolls-Royce was able to return to the private sector.

None of this aircraft engine drama impinged directly on the car division, which was doing well following the 1965 introduction of the all-new and technically advanced Rolls-Royce Silver Shadow and Bentley T-series. At the time of the aero engine disaster, the car division employed about 5,000 people and was believed to be operating profitably (the company never disclosed financial details of the car division) on sales of around 2,000 a year. Its turnover was around £15 million, or about 5 per cent of the group's total. But the aircraft engine issue did have an indirect effect on cars.

David Plastow, a former Vauxhall apprentice who joined Rolls-Royce in 1958, was appointed managing director of the car division on January 1, 1971, a month before the receiver was called in. He was told of the impending development in London shortly before the public announcement. His first task was to rush back to Crewe to announce the news over the Tannoy to the Rolls-Royce workforce before it was formally released.

Rolls-Royce was not the only company in trouble at that time. In 1971, industrialist David Brown finally sold Aston Martin, the sports car company he had financed (at considerable cost) since 1947.

The revelation stunned Rolls-Royce employees everywhere, and not just at Crewe. But they were not totally surprised by the development. Rumours about the RB-211's problems were widespread. And cash requirements for the big aircraft engine project meant the financial noose was tightened across the company. "We were starved of capital in the 1968-69 period," recalled Plastow, who was sales and marketing director of the car division prior to becoming its managing director. "We weren't even allowed to buy the machine tools we needed." Neither was the car division simply allowed to raise its prices, even if it believed its customers would pay more. Any such decision involving the car business required the approval of the full Rolls-Royce board, which comprised almost entirely people with an aero engine background.

The examples illustrate some of the drawbacks associated with diversified industrial groups. Without very strict controls, a problem in one division invariably has an impact on a completely unrelated part of the group. The theme has been repeated so often in the history of the international motor industry it is surprising it retains any currency. Rolls-Royce's aero engine problem became a car division problem, just as tank issues under Vickers shaped Rolls-Royce in a later era. Counter-cyclical diversifications by General Motors, Ford and Chrysler in the 1980s proved disastrous. More recently, the traditionally diversified Fiat group was forced to sell some of its profitable parts because of the commercial and financial problems encountered by the Fiat Auto car-making subsidiary in 2002.

There was much wild speculation about possible outside buyers for the Rolls-Royce car division in 1971. Realistically, though, none of those potential buyers was in a position to take on the complexities and costs involved in owning a car firm. Even car manufacturers shied away because they had no knowledge of making and selling super-expensive vehicles like Rolls-Royces. The only company that did was Ferrari, which itself was obliged to accept financial backing from Fiat only two years before. It would be a different story when Rolls-Royce and Bentley went on the block again two decades later.

Nicholson, the Rolls-Royce receiver, decided to separate the car division with a long-term view to making it fully independent. Just what form that would take was a decision for another day. A new company was formed, Rolls-Royce Motors Ltd, which included the heavy diesel engine operations that supplied commercial vehicle producers and the armed forces. Chief executive Plastow and finance director Tom Neville were the main survivors from the old era. Nicholson later persuaded a City banker and take-over specialist, Ian Fraser, to become chairman. Fraser freely admitted he had no knowledge of the car business. His role was to prepare Rolls-Royce Motors for a possible Stock Exchange listing.

As controller of Rolls-Royce purse strings, Nicholson had to approve all big expenditures. He surprised Plastow by giving the go-ahead for the previously arranged plans for the press launch of the new Corniche convertible, due to take place in the south of France a couple of weeks after the collapse. The launch went well up to the point when Rolls-Royce tried to settle the bill for the hotel just outside Monaco. Such was the international standing of the company that the hotel owner would accept only cash as payment. Rolls-Royce executives somehow managed to collect enough cash between them to pay the bill, but it was an embarrassing reminder of the challenges the newly independent car maker would face with its now diminished status in the world.

Rolls-Royce Motors, with the early quality concerns about the Silver Shadow/T-series solved and the seriously expensive Corniche launched, settled down to a period of profitable stability. The order book was healthy. Nicholson also approved the investment for the Delta project, due to reach the market in 1975 as the Camargue. To counter the inevitable anxiety within the workforces at Crewe and Shrewsbury, where most of the diesel engine business was located, the company introduced monthly meetings at which staff were briefed about business performance and encouraged to put forward their own recommendations. There was concern about the security of their jobs, but there were no redundancies – at that stage.

By the spring of 1973, Nicholson decided Rolls-Royce Motors had reached the point when it could be launched as a private company once more. N.M. Rothschild, the merchant bank, drew up the offer document with a view to obtaining the maximum return for the creditors of the old Rolls-Royce. Substantial offers were believed to have been made by two notable British entrepreneurs of the time,

Tiny Rowland of the Lonrho group and James Hanson of Hanson Trust. Neither was judged an appropriate owner of Rolls-Royce, though it is understood their offers were financially attractive. Indeed, a few days after the public sale of Rolls-Royce Motors in May, Prime Minister Heath told the House of Commons that Rowland and Lonrho represented "an unpleasant and unacceptable face of capitalism" over its mining and trading practices.

Interestingly, there were still no expressions of interest from other vehicle makers. There were probably three particular reasons. First, no company in the world at the time, even giants like General Motors or Ford or prestige car makers like Daimler-Benz and BMW, had any experience of selling what amounted to automotive jewellery. By comparison, a Mercedes-Benz looked like a bargain. The point was echoed by E.M. "Pete" Estes when he was president of General Motors. "You're doing a great job for the industry," he told Plastow. "With the sort of pricing you have for Rolls-Royces, look what we charge for Cadillacs and still look good by comparison."

There was also precious little understanding of the value associated with brands at that time. That had changed by the time Ford bought Jaguar for £1.6 billion nearly two decades later. The price was dictated almost entirely by the image of Jaguar and its potential for development rather than its industrial infrastructure, which was later described by Bill Hayden, the Ford executive assigned to run the company, as the worst car factory he had seen outside the Soviet Union.

Then there was the particularly British nature of the Rolls-Royce and Bentley marques. Consolidation in the British car industry meant that British Leyland was the only group large enough to take on the task, and it was faced with horrendous challenges of its own. They would begin to manifest themselves towards the end of the decade.

If there were no British candidates, how would the public, the politicians and the press react to foreign ownership of these quintessentially British icons? Not very positively, if the reaction to Ford's proposal to buy Land Rover a decade later is any guide. The very idea generated such an emotional public rejection that Ford decided it would be best to walk quietly away from the proposal.

Curiously, the harsh, chauvinistic attitudes towards foreign ownership of traditional British assets changed completely after that. Ford bought Jaguar and Aston Martin in the late 1980s with barely a murmur of protest. When the Rover group, the rump of the old British Leyland conglomerate, was bought by BMW in the early 1990s, the reaction was one of curiosity rather than animosity. And, of course, the sale of Rolls-Royce and Bentley to two German companies in the late 1990s was a cause of sorrow, not spite. No other country in the world would have accepted developments like these with such equanimity. It would certainly not have been the same in France, Germany, Italy or South Korea.

For Nicholson, the solution was to float shares in Rolls-Royce Motors on the London Stock Exchange. The flotation took place on May 10, 1973, 27 months after the parent company's bankruptcy. The share price of 90 pence raised £33 million, an important contribution towards the 20 pence in the pound Nicholson was eventually to achieve for Rolls-Royce's creditors. It was not a particularly popular issue as far as the City was concerned, perhaps because Tony Wedgwood-Benn, the shadow industry secretary during this period, was threatening nationalisation on every front if the Labour Party won the next election. It did, and he didn't.

It was the start of a new era for Rolls-Royce as a vehicle maker, and one it had not experienced since the manufacture of aircraft engines began during the First World War. The company was once more in charge of its own destiny, which it had not been as a division of a group dominated by the business of aircraft engines. While the disciplines of the two sides might have been similar when aeroplanes and cars used internal combustion engines, the arrival of the jet era drove a technology wedge between aero engineers and those making cars. The two sides also had completely different perspectives on development and manufacturing costs. Engineering costs for cars were expensive while those for aircraft engines were astronomical. Even if the separation had not been forced on Rolls-Royce, it seems inevitable that it would have taken place naturally at some later time, just as it did within Fiat, BMW, Daimler-Benz, Saab-Scania, Volvo and Bristol.

Rolls-Royce Motors appeared to be in a healthy position at the flotation. It was profitable and had a relatively new model in the Silver Shadow and a very high-margin derivative in the form of the Corniche. The profit margin on the sale of a Rolls-Royce could be very high, but the company could rely on the sale of only around 2,500 a year. The challenge for the longer term was whether it could generate enough income from those sales to fund the new generation of cars that would be needed in a few years.

Five months later, in October 1973, that task suddenly became much harder, when Egyptian and Syrian forces launched simultaneous attacks on Israel. The Jewish state, backed by the United States, successfully fought back and a ceasefire was achieved four weeks later. But the repercussions of what became known as the Yom Kippur war (it began on the Jewish holy day of that name) were felt globally over the following months after members of the Organisation of Petroleum Exporting Countries quadrupled oil prices and cut production. Energy prices soared, most visibly as motorists queued for scarce, expensive petrol.

Peugeot bought Citroën in 1974. Four years later, Peugeot-Citroën acquired the assets of Chrysler's manufacturing empire in Europe. From its legacy of marques (Simca, Panhard, Darracq, Sunbeam, Hillman, Humber, Singer), the new owners selected Talbot for Chrysler, and then dropped it a few years later.

In Britain, the period covering the end of 1978 and start of 1979 went down in history as the Winter of Discontent in Britain. A festering labour dispute involving coal miners and railway and power station workers erupted in December and resulted in the imposition of a three-day working week as a means of conserving energy stocks. The issue ultimately escalated into a battle over who governed Britain. A general election called by Heath at the end of February produced no clear-cut result, but when Labour's Harold Wilson became prime minister a few days later, his first act was to settle the dispute (at enormous cost) and the country returned to its normal five-day working week.

Britain was not a good place to be doing business at that time, and it was definitely not a good time to be manufacturing very expensive luxury cars that returned 10 or 11 miles per gallon. The imposition of a 50 mph speed limit in order to limit oil imports raised questions about what sort of requirement there would be in the future for cars that could comfortably exceed double that.

The effects of the oil shock took its toll across the motor industry in the mid-1970s, as global demand slumped, stocks of unsold cars built up and factory-manning levels were cut, sometimes permanently. Global car production, having risen steadily over the previous two decades, dropped from a peak of just under 30 million in 1973 to below 25 million two years later. Aston Martin was forced to halt production pending the sale of the company. It led to the collapse of another famous British marque, Jensen. Citroën abandoned its control of Maserati in Italy, and was itself subsequently taken over by rival Peugeot. Ferrucio Lamborghini sold his shareholding in the high-performance car company he had created only a decade before and turned instead to making wine.

The general slump in business in the car industry had further complications. Ever since an activist lawyer named Ralph Nader published his book, *Unsafe at any Speed*, in 1965, there had been great pressure on vehicle makers to produce cars that held the road better and gave better protection to their passengers in the event of a crash. That added to their development costs. In addition, the gathering pace of exhaust emissions legislation coming out of the United States, and particularly the standards set by the California Air Resources Board, required a huge allocation of research and development funds for any company wanting to sell in America.

Volkswagen signalled the beginning of a new era when it launched the modern, front-wheel-drive Golf in autumn

1974. The car became an instant best-seller, just like the famous rear-engined, rear-drive Beetle, which continued in production outside Europe for many more years.

At Rolls-Royce, a company whose future depended on its presence in the world's wealthiest and largest car market, it required enormous enterprise and endeavour on the part of the small engineering team, led by chief engineer John Hollings. It also meant the company had to allocate half its R&D budget simply to make sure its cars complied with US legislation. The focus on energy conservation after the oil crisis then required Rolls-Royce to devote extra attention to making its cars more economical.

This was the harsh commercial environment faced by Rolls-Royce Motors within months of achieving its independence. On the face of it, then, the launch of the enormous Camargue two-door coupé in March 1975 did not seem like the key to the company's future. However, Rolls-Royce had been committed to the car long before the events of autumn 1973. As it turned out, the Camargue proved a particularly cost-effective way of raising profit margins, and interest in other models in the range, for a relatively modest outlay in development and tooling.

The unusual-looking Camargue was designed by Pininfarina and cost around £30,000, or twice as much as the Silver Shadow on which it was based. Like the Corniche before it, the model quickly found favour among faithful Rolls-Royce customers, particularly in the United States. A waiting list built up. While the company was able to satisfy only one or two orders a week, the Camargue's appearance in dealer showrooms proved a sales stimulus for other Rolls-Royces which could be delivered more quickly.

This approach worked surprisingly well for Rolls-Royce as global sales recovered in the second half of the 1970s. However, the board recognised that a more substantial overhaul of its range was necessary for the longer term. When the board members gathered for their 1977 strategy review, the Silver Shadow was already 12 years old. In car industry terms, the model was almost at the end of its technological (and sales) life cycle, especially with the advances for passenger cars promised by new electronic controls. Based on the belief that the small market in which Rolls-Royce competed was not about to die, the board decided to fund the development of a new range to replace the Silver Shadow and T-series.

Even to be able to do so was quite an achievement considering the turmoil to which Rolls-Royce was subjected after its independence: the sudden sales slump after the 1973 oil crisis and the cost of meeting new emissions and safety legislation. But a new range was a priority. "Even to pause would have been dangerous," Plastow reflected in 2003.

CHAPTER 10

ALL CHANGE

Two events in 1980 were pivotal in the history of Rolls-Royce Motors. It was the year the 15-year-old Silver Shadow and T-series were replaced by the Silver Spirit and Mulsanne. And it was the year the Vickers engineering group finally got its hands on Rolls-Royce, or at least the car-making part of it. Two or three years into the decade, there must have been many occasions when Vickers wished it had not bothered.

Vickers, with origins dating back to the second half of the 19th century, was down on its luck by the time of the merger with Rolls-Royce Motors. It was once the Krupp of Britain, the nation's pre-eminent arms manufacturer. However, true to its election promise, the Labour government nationalised Vickers' core ship and aircraft-building interests in 1977. With its heart ripped out, Vickers was in an invidious position. It could not undertake any new business initiatives while questions about the final size and timing of its compensation were still being argued over with the government, a process that continued for years.

The group still made tanks and armoured vehicles, but its other interests ranged across office furniture, printing plates, machine tools, metal coatings, medical equipment and marine engineering. Much of it was journeyman work that could be done more cheaply in developing countries. There were no obvious synergies between the businesses, a point acknowledged by the two companies when the merger proposal was revealed in June 1980. The aim was to turn two smallish engineering companies into one larger one better able to weather the peaks and troughs of business cycles. The reaction was lukewarm. "A marriage of convenience between two members of the squirearchy that have fallen on hard times," noted Hamish McRae in the *Guardian*. Patrick Sargeant, in a reference to a then-fashionable night-club in London's West End, wrote in the *Daily Mail* that the merger "looks nothing so much as two dukes falling upstairs out of Annabel's, propping each other up".

The secret merger negotiations began four weeks earlier under the appropriate code name of War and Peace. The basis for the proposal, announced at the London headquarters of Vickers' bankers, Morgan Grenfell, and subsequently approved by both sets of shareholders, was one ordinary Vickers share (suspended at 129 pence) for two Rolls-Royce Motors shares at 60 pence each. That was a third below the level at which Rolls-Royce was floated seven years earlier.

Sir Peter Matthews, the Vickers chairman, became chairman of the unified group. Rolls-Royce chairman Ian Fraser was deputy chairman and Plastow, managing director of Rolls-Royce and a non-executive director of Vickers since 1975, stepped up to be the chief executive. When the merger was proposed, Vickers had debts of around £100 million against shareholder funds of £171 million, though that was expected to be reduced through future disposals. Rolls-Royce's debts were £45 million, equivalent to 70 per cent of shareholder funds.

Rolls-Royce, which raised money through two rights issues after its market introduction, was short of cash because of the imminent launch of its new range of cars, scheduled for that October's motor show in Paris. Neither had the late 1970s been kind to the company. Rolls-Royce was handicapped by a malaise in the diesel engine market and general industrial unrest in Britain's engineering sector. It then suffered a serious set-back when a huge order for diesel engines and spares from the Ministry of Defence was cancelled. The engines were destined for installation in main battle tanks to be delivered to Iran. The order was effectively cancelled when the Iranian revolution led by Ayatollah Ruhollah Khomeini forced the Shah into exile in January 1979. Once again, events in the Middle East were to send energy prices around the world skywards.

The popularity of economical and reliable little cars by Japanese vehicle makers shot up in the 1970s and 1980s. When US and European manufacturers began to suffer, Japan began to build localised factories that came to be known as "transplants". The first was Honda's in Ohio in 1982. Many others followed in North America and Europe.

However, Rolls-Royce cars, which accounted for around 70 per cent of the company's sales, were never more popular. With a low mileage secondhand Silver Shadow changing hands for more than the list price of a new one, ownership of a Rolls-Royce became an investment. Car sales in 1978 reached 3,347. This level was not achieved again for 12 years, and never again by the time the two marques were separated at the end of 2002. Even so, sales were well over 3,000 in 1979, dipped below 2,900 during the model change-over the following year, and then climbed back to over 3,200 in 1981, the first full year of availability of the new generation cars. The outlook was excellent. Rolls-Royce management talked confidently of 3,500 car sales the following year (1982) and of even reaching 5,000 a year towards the end of the decade.

It may have looked like that in Crewe, but the reality was rather different. Starting in 1982, Rolls-Royce's annual sales dipped below 2,400 and stayed there for the following three years. An almost overnight drop in business of 25 per cent was a serious blow to a small company like Rolls-Royce, and for the group that had only recently bought it. The inevitable happened. Most of the top management was changed and employment at Rolls-Royce was cut from around 6,600 in 1981 to 4,500 two years later. Those people who remained were put on a short working week in an effort to adjust output to demand. A five-week strike at Crewe, the first in 23 years, was staged in autumn 1983.

The fall-off in demand for Rolls-Royces came against a back-ground of general economic slowdown and higher energy prices. The decline, which was particularly pronounced in Rolls-Royce's two primary markets, Britain and the United States, was self-perpetuating. The *Financial Times* quoted one company director as saying, "It's just not diplomatic to drive the new Rolls past the bulletin board which posts the latest redundancy notices." But the issue was not just one for luxury manufacturers. Car makers everywhere were laying off staff and announcing redundancies. The outlook for Chrysler Corporation, under new chairman Lee Iacocca, was so poor that it was forced to beg the government for federal loan guarantees, money Iacocca proudly repaid seven years early. In Britain, Michael Edwardes was dismantling the unwieldy monster that was BL. It involved the closure or sale of dozens of factories and businesses.

New political thinking made state ownership of car makers unfashionable in the 1980s. Volkswagen began the process of buying Seat from the Spanish state's INI holding company. Alfa Romeo, for many decades under the ownership of Italy's IRI, was bought by Fiat after a bitter battle with Ford. And Jaguar, once part of nationalised BL, was privatised and then bought by Ford.

Rolls-Royce's new generation models made their debuts in Paris less than five months after the idea of the merger with Vickers became public knowledge. The Silver Spirit replaced the Silver Shadow and the Mulsanne replaced the T-series. There was also a long wheelbase version known as the Silver Spur, effectively a 1980s equivalent of the old Silver Wraith. The cars were developed as a result of a £28 million investment, a very large sum for a company of Rolls-Royce's scale but barely enough for new door handles for a mass-produced model. The Silver Spirit series therefore used many components from the second generation of its predecessors, including the 6.75-litre V8 engine, three-speed General Motors automatic transmission, front and rear suspension, steering, and bi-level air conditioning. Like the Silver Shadow, the new model's unitary body was built by Pressed Steel Fisher in Oxford. The newcomer was lower, a little longer and wider, and around 10 per cent heavier than the Silver Shadow.

What distinguished the Silver Spirit was its body shape, designed by Fritz Feller. An Austrian refugee who arrived in Britain in 1939 and joined Rolls-Royce as an apprentice, Feller was something of a Renaissance man. His background was mainly as a gas turbine engineer. He transferred to the car division to work on the company's experimental Wankel twin-rotary known as the "cottage loaf" engine. An accomplished painter and musician, Feller then made another unusual career move by transferring to the design department to replace John Blatchley.

The Silver Spirit was clearly in the traditions of the company, but it featured larger windows, a lower waistline, a neater rear end and a shallower radiator shell with softer edges. At the time of the car's launch, Feller spoke about his design philosophy for Rolls-Royce: "Nothing in this world is so dull and miserable as the 'average' or 'the mean'. Once we throw away the concept of excellence and perfection we take away the excitement for living. That is why we at Rolls-Royce must always remain true to our best traditions." His words could easily have been spoken by the company's co-founder, Sir Henry Royce.

It was accepted within the company that the Silver Shadow's life cycle of 15 years was far too long. The car had been overtaken in engineering terms by other manufacturers, and to buyers it looked tired towards the end. Thus, the Silver Spirit series, developed as it was from the Silver Shadow, was expected to have a life cycle in the region of 10 years. As it turned out, the basic design was not replaced until 1998, or 18 years after its launch.

In other words, 33 years elapsed between the appearance of the original Silver Shadow and the final Silver Spirit whispering out of Crewe. It was far too long for any product that wished to retain its status as "the best in the world". During a period of that length, Mercedes-Benz and BMW, Rolls-Royce's closest rivals in prestige car terms, were able to pack in three cycles for their premium models. This was when Rolls-Royce began failing to live up to the famous slogan rightly acquired during its formative years: the best car in the world. The Rolls-Royce myth could no longer match the reality.

The reason is not the rather shallow one of change for the sake of change, although design preferences mean today's products are nothing like those of 20 years ago, whether they are coats or cookers, shoes or sofas. The latest examples are not necessarily better visually; they are just different. Fashion is a fleeting fancy. The car industry, on the other hand, underwent a major technological revolution during the last quarter of the 20th century. As it did so, Rolls-Royce remained trapped in a time warp.

Cars today are not laboriously designed on drawing boards, as they once were. They are products of computers that can instantly calculate exact panel gaps, wheel travel movements and body integrity. They can predict how a car will deform in a crash and when a component will fail. Modern cars are made of materials that are lighter, stronger and more durable than anything that went before. Their functions are controlled precisely by electronics for better fuel consumption, lower emissions and smoother running. They are manufactured with an automated precision never previously possible, thanks to computer-controlled transfer presses, body-framing jigs and assembly robots. By contrast, low volumes meant the Silver Spirit's body shell was still made by hand and eye co-ordination methods at Oxford.

Technological breakthroughs tend to be introduced into a factory production system or product line only when a model is renewed, which, outside Rolls-Royce, ranges from four to eight years. The result is that during the three decades of inertia when the Silver Shadow and Silver Spirit were in production, a steady flow of new technology transformed the high-volume family car and the way it is made. It is as comfortable, quiet, spacious and reliable today as yesterday's exclusive luxury car. Of course, it returns better mileage and produces fewer emissions. And it costs a great deal less to buy in real terms. The extent of this advance can be understood by comparing cars of then and now. Just after the Silver Shadow was launched, the family cars of the day in Britain were models such as the Austin Maxi and Ford Cortina. When the Silver Spirit was at the end of its life, the mass-market equivalents were the Renault Megane and Ford Mondeo. The engineering and design links between the Silver Shadow and Silver Spirit are clear. There are no such connections between a Maxi and a Megane.

The stimulus for many of the changes were the manufacturing and quality standards set by Japanese vehicle makers, which began winning new customers around the world in the 1970s and 1980s. They did so to such an alarming degree that, in order to stay in business, their rivals in North America and Europe had to improve. Painfully and gradually, they did. The result is that the quality and reliability – but not the longevity – of today's modest Hondas, Fords and Renaults are on a par with those of Rolls-Royces costing 10 times more. That was definitely not the case in the past.

The family car business may have had nothing to do with the rarefied world of the ultimate luxury car maker, but what happened had a "trickle-up" effect on every company involved in the industry. Rolls-Royce's lofty perspective had to change when similar things happened within companies that already had excellent global reputations. In engineering, quality, safety and performance terms, the Mercedes-Benz S-class, BMW 7-series and Audi A8 were every bit a match for a Rolls-Royce, at half the price. So, from the end of the 1980s, were the top Lexus models created by Toyota. Of course, none of them had those pinnacles of prestige, the interlocked double-R or winged B badges. The scramble for those did not take place until the end of the century.

So, mass production proved the great leveller in the late 20th century, which was why little Rolls-Royce, unable to afford these new developments, saw its advantages in product quality eroded, and in some cases exceeded. Its designs, its systems, were overtaken by events.

Despite that, Rolls-Royce did a remarkable job within the budgets it had. Its cars were updated, improved and refined. At the same time, its development budgets faced the demand occasioned by the need to comply with ever-tougher emissions, safety and noise legislation. There was also the additional cost that flowed from the eminently sensible decision to resurrect the somnolent Bentley brand. It cost money to create the appropriate Bentley products and to make sure the world knew they were available.

However impressively Rolls-Royce managed to juggle its money, and however large its spending as a proportion of annual income, its budgets in absolute terms were insignificant. Peter Ward, who became chief executive in 1986, noted that in one year in the late 1980s Rolls-Royce's turnover was around £240 million while the R&D budget at Mercedes-Benz was £250 million. It was a sober reminder of the scale of the challenges faced by a small, independent car maker in the late 20th century.

Meanwhile, Vickers' new management tried to bring more focus to the group following the merger. The car-making side of Rolls-Royce and tank-building were safe, but Vickers began a series of company disposals and made a number of acquisitions. It embraced the philosophy that, if a business could not genuinely compete with the leading companies in the sector (many of them Japanese at the time), Vickers would sell it. It was akin to the theory successfully employed by Jack Welch to build GE in the United States: be No.1 or No.2 in a sector, or get out. Developments a few years later saw Vickers take the philosophy to its ultimate conclusion.

Vickers made 11 sales, including its interests in mining equipment in South Africa and shipbuilding in Australia. Printing plates, furniture and metal treatment went. So did the diesel engine business at Shrewsbury that was part of Rolls-Royce's marriage dowry. When the legendary Arnold Weinstock was asked whether his British GE group would be interested in the business, he wanted to know whether it made any money. "Some, not much," he was told truthfully. "Don't want it," was the quick, clipped Weinstock verdict. The former Rolls-Royce diesel business was sold to Perkins Engines, which itself became part of Caterpillar.

As part of its mission to build a stable group, Vickers bought and developed KaMeWa, a ship propulsion specialist, and Ross Catherall, which made alloys for the aerospace sector. It bought Riva, the Italian boat-building firm frequently described as the luxury marine market's equivalent of Rolls-Royce. The Riva purchase was not a success, however. The company cost Vickers very little to buy, but it was in need of a lot of investment and a restructuring that would have been difficult under Italian labour laws. The vision was to pair Riva with Fairline, the highly respected boat-builder based in Oundle, England, which Vickers was also considering buying at the time. It did not happen.

When a better business opportunity presented itself, Vickers backed away from the Fairline idea and later sold Riva. The new opportunity was the purchase from Carlton Communications of Cosworth Engineering, a world-leader in the development and production of high-performance engines for racing and road cars. Cosworth, based in Northampton, was founded in 1958. Its roots were in international motor sport, where Cosworth engines were regular winners in Formula One and CART racing. At the time Vickers bought it for £163.5 million in March 1990, Cosworth's road car customers included Ford, General Motors and Mercedes-Benz.

For Plastow, who was knighted in 1986 for services to export, being chief executive of Vickers meant he had to step back from the day-to-day business of Rolls-Royce. That was hard for a man whose whole career had been in the motor industry, starting with an apprenticeship at General Motors' British subsidiary, Vauxhall. Complicating Rolls-Royce's problems was that, just as Plastow was taking up his primary duties at the Vickers group, the economic slump of the early 1980s sent demand for luxury cars into a downward spiral. It was clear Rolls-Royce needed more help. A new top team, mostly recruited from outside Rolls-Royce, was brought in at Crewe. They were presented with plenty of challenges, but it quickly became clear that Rolls-Royce was wasting one of its most valuable assets: Bentley. They set about rebuilding Bentley with a proper product range, not just as re-badged Rolls-Royces.

CHAPTER 11

BENTLEY COMES IN FROM THE COLD

By the end of the 1970s, Bentley was like the great star player who had prematurely and unaccountably been left on the substitutes' bench. Bentley was a talent wasted, ignored for the best part of two decades to the point when the only differences between a Silver Shadow and a T-series were the designs of the grille and wheels. One senior executive of the time recalled opening the bonnet of a nearly completed Bentley on the Crewe production line to find Rolls-Royce labels on the engine's rocker covers. Benign neglect had gone too far.

And yet, it was not always so. The first model manufactured at Crewe when it was converted from aircraft engine production to cars after the Second World War was a Bentley Mk VI. The Bentley range fitted the grim reality of post-war austerity in Britain much better than the Rolls-Royce Silver Wraith series. It was believed that Rolls-Royces were just too opulent and ostentatious at a time of rationing and reconstruction. This was reflected in the output of Mk VIs which out-numbered Silver Wraiths by four-to-one by the time both series went out of production in the second half of the 1950s.

That was the era of the model epitomising Bentley elegance and understatement: the Continental Type R of 1952-55. It was entirely fitting that Ian Fleming, when he created the James Bond character in his spy novels published around that time, should put his hero behind the wheel of a Continental. The two-door coupé, based on the Mk VI chassis, was reputed to be the fastest four-seater of its day, with a top speed of around 115 mph. Most Continentals were fitted with the peerless fast-back body designed and built by H.J. Mulliner. It became a classic shape, to which Dirk van Braeckel turned for inspiration when he began designing the 2003 Continental GT.

The marque was still a large element of the Silver Cloud and S-series that followed. Bentley's versions, including a few Mulliner-bodied Continental Ss that replicated the original R, accounted for just under half of all output while the series was in production during 1955-64.

Bentley then virtually disappeared. It is particularly incomprehensible today that a flagship model like the Continental was simply abandoned. The last one was made in 1959, and yet the chassis on which it was based was in production for another six years. The Silver Shadow and T-series, with their unitary construction, arrived in 1965 and departed in 1980. During that period, only 7 per cent of the combined output comprised Bentleys. By the end, the Bentley element was 3 per cent. The Silver Spirit and Mulsanne, which carried over most of the engineering features of their predecessors, seemed destined to continue the trend when introduced in 1980. However, the very worrying sales slump at the start of the decade and the appointment at Crewe of some new decision-makers who had not been moulded by the mores of Rolls-Royce culture, set the stage for a Bentley revival.

David Plastow acknowledges he "got a lot of stick" about what happened to Bentley during his watch. "What people forget is that we went bust in 1971. Our priority was to get Rolls-Royce back on track, and I still think that was the right thing to do at the time," he said in early 2003. For Plastow, that meant selling lots of cars in the United States. It was, and is, the world's largest market for luxury cars, but it was also one in which the Bentley name was virtually unknown. Emphasising Rolls-Royce gave the company the sales volumes it needed to stay in business.

When Plastow moved to Vickers after the 1980 merger, George

Fenn, whose background was in the car maker's purchasing department, became Rolls-Royce's chief executive. Demand for Rolls-Royces had never been better than over the previous few years, there was a new range to sell (the Silver Spirit), and the outlook appeared promising. However, Fenn's world was about to collapse.

The sharp contraction in demand for Rolls-Royces in the middle of 1982 was not an aberration. The slump had already hit the makers of mass-market cars, but Rolls-Royce was cushioned from its effect for several months by the wealth of its customers. But Britain was a country in the kind of debilitating turmoil not conducive to the sale of expensive cars. It went to war with Argentina to reverse the invasion of the Falkland Islands in 1982. The continuing troubles in Northern Ireland exploded onto the mainland in October 1984 when the IRA attempted to assassinate Prime Minister Thatcher by blowing up the Grand Hotel, Brighton. The civil unrest during the year-long miners' strike of 1984-85 came against a background of perpetual protest about the installation of cruise missiles at Greenham Common. Once down, sales by the Rolls-Royce company stayed low for four years and did not return to their pre-crisis levels until 1989. When they did, it was on the strength of Bentley rather than Rolls-Royce.

John DeLorean's scheme to build gull-winged sports cars in Belfast came to a sudden halt in February 1982 when the company went into receivership. Untangling the affair dragged on for years.

When the crisis began, Vickers decided drastic changes were required at Rolls-Royce. Fenn took early retirement in May 1984 and was replaced by Dick Perry. A former Leyland manufacturing man, Perry had been put in charge of production at Crewe after running Rolls-Royce's Mulliner-Park Ward coachbuilding subsidiary in north London.

Perry was joined in February 1983 by two other outsiders destined to change the way Rolls-Royce did business: Mike Dunne as engineering director and Peter Ward as sales and marketing director. They immediately realised that Rolls-Royce lacked a fundamental that is taken for granted in all other car companies: a proper idea of the types and numbers of cars the company expected to sell over the coming years. When they recruited John Stephenson from the Rover group later that year, he became Rolls-Royce's first ever product planning director.

Dunne was a graduate engineer at Ford before becoming chief engineer of Alvis in the 1960s, just like his father before him. By coincidence, Ward's father had also been an engineer at Alvis. When the Coventry producer gave up the struggle to stay in car production, Dunne moved to Leyland and in 1973 re-joined his first employer, Ford. By the time he moved to Rolls-Royce, Dunne had risen through the engineering ranks at Ford to take overall responsibility for the Sierra, a critical saloon that took the company in a new direction. At Rolls-Royce, his mission was to modernise the products and to introduce some Ford-style cost controls.

They were needed. Rolls-Royce's engineering department did wonderful work that was a credit to the company's traditions. But it was a law to itself. It produced what it judged best for the company and not necessarily what was best for the market. It was an unreal world harking back to a time when Rolls-Royce could sell every car it could build and customers were prepared to wait for delivery. With new competitive pressures, this was no longer the case. Rolls-Royce met all its critical projects – those that involved legislative requirements – but others lacked discipline. It was not the same at other car companies, where the aims of a project were defined, a budget set, and a timetable agreed. If none of this happened according to plan, the repercussions for the company, the department, and the personnel involved were dire.

It is difficult not to conclude that attitudes in Rolls-Royce's vehicle engineering department were shaped when its parent company was primarily a defence contractor. By their nature, defence contractors the world over are almost obliged to run behind schedule and over budget while failing to meet performance targets, safe in the knowledge that their governments will bail them out. It is as true today as it was in the past. When the car division was separated after the 1971 collapse – itself rooted in an ill-conceived civilian contract agreed by engineers – the old Rolls-Royce ways of thinking went with it.

The extent of engineering's influence at Rolls-Royce can be gauged by the fact that, true to the company's long history of manufacturing as much as possible in-house, the car company still manufactured its own nuts and bolts up to 1985. It did this despite the easy availability of what was a basic manufacturing commodity from GKN. As a supplier whose origins were as a nuts and bolts producer, GKN could offer them at a fraction of the price it cost Rolls-Royce to make their own. Rolls-Royce also cadmium-plated its own components, including those that were hidden, instead of giving the job to a specialist company. Consumer tastes in car ride, handling and road-holding had also been re-shaped by the latest breed of prestige models from BMW and Mercedes-Benz, and also from Audi and Jaguar. They felt tauter and sharper than a Rolls-Royce, which retained the floaty ride, ultra-light steering and pronounced cornering-roll that customers in the United States seemed to like. Rolls-Royce was being true to its traditions, but the world had moved on. Dunne's role was to edge the company forward without alienating existing owners.

Ward was Dunne's opposite number on the commercial side. He, too, spent his career in the wider motor industry before moving to Rolls-Royce. His first job was as a service liaison representative at Standard-Triumph in 1967. During the era of British Leyland consolidation, he became parts sales manager at Jaguar Rover Triumph and then commercial manager at Unipart. He switched to Talbot (the former Chrysler and Rootes operations) to become managing director of its Motaquip parts company in 1979 before taking the trip to Crewe four years later.

Ward was put in charge of Rolls-Royce's global sales and marketing, before going to become the company's chief executive and the reviver of Bentley. It would clearly be a difficult task to get the company out of its sales rut. The enthusiasm for Rolls-Royces in the late 1970s had given way to indifference. The products were considered fuddy-duddy. They were purchased by old money. The new money created by Reaganomics in the United States and Thatcherism in Britain favoured BMW, Mercedes-Benz and Porsche. The time was right for a Bentley revival.

However, that could not be achieved overnight. The immediate problem was that new Rolls-Royces were much less socially desirable. If it was unable to sell enough new ones, the company decided its dealers needed support in selling secondhand ones. It began an unprecedented advertising campaign that promoted used cars by emphasising their low depreciation rates. The general theme was, "You'll love it. Your accountant will like it even better". It enjoyed some success, but Rolls-Royce as a brand was on its way to being eclipsed by Bentley.

A turbocharged version of the Bentley Mulsanne, distinguished by the adoption of a body-coloured radiator grille rather than a chrome one, was introduced in March 1982. Exhaust-driven turbocharging to produce very high-performance cars was a deliberate echo of the Bentleys with mechanically driven superchargers that enjoyed so much motor racing success in the 1920s and 1930s.

The origins of the project date back to the previous decade. Because of the pressure on Rolls-Royce's engineering department to meet emissions and safety legislation at the time, the initial development contract for turbocharging the company's V8 engine was handed to Broadspeed, then a very successful saloon car racing team and engine-tuning firm. The development car was perfected at Crewe and became the Bentley Turbo. It was very fast, but not that refined, and was prone to starting problems when hot. None was sold outside Bentley's home market.

But it was the foundation stone for the Bentley revival and the kick-start for the marque came with the arrival of the new top management team the following year. Ward, in particular, was most closely associated with the strategy of rescuing Bentley from oblivion. Ward became the company's managing director in October 1986 and its chief executive the following April when Perry followed Fenn into retirement. The actions he and his fellow board members took during the mid-1980s would have far-reaching financial implications for Vickers and for Volkswagen when Rolls-Royce and Bentley were put up for sale towards the end of 1997. Without the start of the Bentley revival, it is difficult to imagine Volkswagen paying as much as it did for the company.

The new team decided to broaden Bentley's market appeal beyond the new Mulsanne and ageing Corniche, which it renamed Continental. Its first product action was bold; to offer a more afford-able Bentley. It carried the danger of damaging Bentley's classy image, as well as eroding profit margins. The resulting Eight saloon was definitely not cheap when it was launched in the middle of 1984, however. Based on the Mulsanne, it featured a lower specification interior and stiffer front suspension. It was distinguished by a bright wire-mesh grille that picked up on a design feature of the first Bentleys. The Eight went on sale at approximately £49,500, or 10 per cent less than the Mulsanne.

Transport of a different type was offered to British consumers in the spring of 1985. But Clive Sinclair's battery-powered Sinclair C5 single-seater, built in a Hoover factory in Wales, disappeared from the market shortly after it was launched.

In the spring of the following year, the Turbo R replaced the rather deficient Turbo. It proved a turning point for Bentley. The R had a stiffened body shell – later used for Rolls-Royces as well – far more dynamic handling properties and sporty body-styling modifi-cations, the work of the young head of design at the MGA consultan-cy in Coventry, Peter Horbury. He went on to become the leading designer at Volvo, and was later put in charge of all brands within Ford's Premier Automotive Group, including Aston Martin, Jaguar and Land Rover. The R was initially fitted with a Solex four-barrel car-burettor like its predecessor, but was equipped with Bosch fuel injec-tion the following year to produce 385 horsepower. The company claimed it was the fastest-accelerating saloon car in the world.

Another event that year gave a clear indication of the new Rolls-

Royce management's thinking about Bentley. At the Geneva motor show in March, the company displayed a stylish glassfibre mock-up that it referred to as Project 90, a two-door coupé based on the Turbo R. The public reaction to Project 90 was sufficiently positive for the company to press ahead with a development programme and to undertake more market research. Work progressed well, although Ward began to have reservations because he thought the project's test mule – referred to internally as the Black Rat because of its colour – looked too much like a Lincoln Continental coupé and would date very quickly unless it could be launched within 18 months.

This proved to be the dividing issue when the board of Rolls-Royce met in 1987 to decide whether Project 90 should go into production. The added problem was that, even if the car could be made production-ready within that time-frame, Rolls-Royce's manufacturing structure was too dysfunctional to produce it.

With restricted financial resources, the board changed tack. Instead of making the investment in order to get Project 90 to market quickly, it decided to sort out its production system. There was one dissenting voice. Stephenson, the product planner who was recruited specifically to come up with future models like Project 90, was bitterly disappointed. In a dramatic gesture, he flung a black plastic rat on to the table as he announced his resignation.

The result was that Project 90 died that day and Rolls-Royce began to address its manufacturing issues. Any new models would have to come later, but they would benefit from Rolls-Royce's new manufacturing processes. Meanwhile, it commissioned its two designers, Ken Greenley and John Heffernan, to come up with some ideas for a replacement for the highly profitable Rolls-Royce Corniche. Although it was introduced in 1971, the Corniche had maintained its popularity in the United States, but that could not last much longer. A replacement was overdue.

The two designers, both lecturers on the internationally acclaimed automotive design course at the Royal College of Art in London, started from the beginning once more. They concentrated on a Rolls-Royce version, but simultaneously produced a more muscular, sporty edition to carry a Bentley badge. When the Rolls-Royce board came to review the full-size split clay model – one half Rolls-Royce, the other Bentley – it quickly became clear which way it would vote. The result of its deliberation was finally unveiled at the Geneva motor show in March 1991. The Continental R became the first Bentley to benefit from a dedicated design since the old Continental of 1959.

The car, which used a body shell fabricated by Park Sheet Metal in Coventry, was brought to market for an expenditure (mainly on tooling) of only £19 million. It became the most expensive model in the company's range at £175,000 following the axing of the Camargue in 1986. The most expensive, that is, until the convertible version, the Azure, arrived in 1995 priced at approximately £215,000. The Continental R was an instant hit. From an initial expectation that orders would require construction of seven cars a week, the company was forced to raise output to the maximum of 12 a week.

The combination of the cheaper Eight, the faster Turbo R, and the resurrection of the legendary Continental name for the flagship model, successfully re-established Bentley as a distinct brand within Rolls-Royce Motor Cars (as the company became in 1986), and as a new competitor in the prestige car sector. The Turbo R, once it was equipped with fuel injection, exceeded all sales expectations in two important markets where the brand was virtually unknown, the United States and Japan.

The term "Bentley Motors" began to be used as a separate name once more. The marque began the 1980s in virtual oblivion, but the switch in strategic emphasis meant that 52 per cent of the group's global sales by 1990 were Bentleys. Neither did it stop there. The proportion was up to 61 per cent by 1995 and 73 per cent when the new millennium began. What the trend also indicates, of course, is that demand for Rolls-Royces began heading for oblivion. The irony is that Rolls-Royce Motor Cars survived the last two decades of the 20th century by reviving the brand that it spent the previous two decades ignoring. It was the period when Bentley rescued Rolls-Royce – a *de facto* reversal of the take-over of 1931.

CHAPTER 12

ONE CRISIS TOO MANY FOR VICKERS

R olls-Royce's new management realised that bringing Bentley back to life would not solve the company's more fundamental problems. The shock of the parent group's bankruptcy, the period of private ownership and the merger with Vickers occurred within less than a decade. Car sales that had soared to unprecedented levels in the late 1970s sank to unsustainably low numbers, in spite of the new range launched in 1980. The actual production numbers, normally more or less in line with sales, were much worse because of a build-up of unsold stocks. The headline figure of 3,200 sales in 1981 masked the reality that production was under half that. The pay strike of late 1983 came against a background of short-time working and substantial redundancies.

Rolls-Royce Motors was a demoralised company. The proud and skilled workforce at Crewe, where the town signs proclaimed it was the "home of the best car in the world", had trouble adjusting to the concept of rejection. Indeed, there was a double blow for the town, which had been a major centre of the railway industry since the early 19th century. Until the arrival of Rolls-Royce at the end of the 1930s, Crewe and the railway were so synonymous that they were bowdlerised in popular song and comedy. But the town's enormous British Rail engineering works, one of the largest yards of its type in Europe, was under threat at around the same time as Rolls-Royce's troubles. The steady run-down of the railway works, which employed thousands of highly qualified designers, engineers and fitters, began in the early 1980s. The great yard was a shadow of its former size by the start of the 21st century. The little left of the once-great works was owned by Bombardier, the Canadian transport group. The remainder of the site comprised huge tracts of derelict, brick-strewn land and boarded-up buildings, criss-crossed by empty, crumbling streets.

Rolls-Royce was being pulled in all directions. As income from sales plummeted, it still had to address the requirements of emissions and safety legislation coming out of its two main markets, the United States and Europe, which set standards for the UK. Those were paramount. At the same time, it was attempting to breathe life into a moribund Bentley. As for the electronically controlled features that bigger, wealthier companies managed to bring to market, little Rolls-Royce did not have the engineering budgets, the resources or the experience to develop them. Technologically, it was out of its depth in an era when the car was undergoing a revolution. The simple metal box (invariably steel) adorned by a few electronic add-on components was being transformed into a hugely complex electronic device held together by a metal box (increasingly aluminium). To develop cars, algorithms became as important as Ackermann angles.

There was a growing realisation within the company that Rolls-Royce would eventually have to go into partnership with a large car maker. But that was not for the moment. In the meanwhile, it decided to sub-contract most of the development work on electronically controlled components like fuel injection, anti-lock brakes, air bags and automatic ride height to the industry's leading suppliers such as Siemens and Bosch. The penalty was that it paid a higher unit price than a company like BMW, for example, which had the resources to do much of the work itself as well as being in a position to place monthly orders in thousands rather than hundreds. For a company with a pricing structure like Rolls-Royce, however, the cost of bought-in components was less critical.

By 1984, with overheads reduced and demand for its cars beginning to recover, Rolls-Royce became cash positive once more. The bull market of the late 1980s ensured it remained so until the end of the decade. The expanding economies of the late 1980s in the United States, Britain and Japan generated many new "high net worth" consumers, as they were defined, well able to order Rolls-Royces, and increasingly Bentleys. Even Black Monday, the day stock markets crashed around the world in October 1987, was not as bad as it first looked. Stocks recovered and sales of Rolls-Royces quickly resumed. Demand rose steadily from 2,270 in 1984 to 3,333 in 1990, fractionally below the 3,347 achieved in 1978.

The car maker used the improved income stream to fund engineering's legislative requirements and the Bentley revival. The company also had another useful source of income, little known outside the factory gates. Rolls-Royce continued to fulfil certain unidentified orders from the Ministry of Defence right up to the point when Vickers sold the company to Volkswagen. People who worked on the Crewe site knew Rolls-Royce's buildings were painted grey, and those of the ministry were khaki.

But, as a small company, Rolls-Royce budgets were limited. Towards the end of the decade, it elected to tackle Crewe's rather chaotic parts and production system rather than rush the Bentley Project 90 concept to market. The decision caught many within Rolls-Royce by surprise. After having its agenda set for years by engineers, the company was suddenly being led by Ward, a sales and marketing specialist. The priority might have been expected to be a series of attractive new models to keep the dealers happy. Instead, the company addressed the basics by implementing a new manufacturing structure. Rolls-Royce put in a system of manufacturing planning processes known as MRP2. It proved complex and time-consuming to install properly, but eventually gave the company control over component flows and work in progress where almost none existed previously. A new paint plant to comply with the latest emissions standards was installed in 1989 at a cost of £12 million. With a capacity of 5,000 jobs a year, Rolls-Royce offered its facilities for painting low-volume models such as Aston Martins and Rover's revived MGB sports cars.

Rolls-Royce also negotiated with employees to dispense with the time-honoured practice of piecework in favour of bonuses based on output. In another change that would have been unthinkable in the hierarchical structure of Rolls-Royce a few years earlier, the three separate canteens for line workers, foremen and managers were amalgamated into one. It also negotiated an agreement to reduce the number of trades unions at Crewe from 13 to three. A class system as stratified as the cars built at Crewe was beginning to modernise.

After a very difficult start to the 1980s, Rolls-Royce began to do well as the decade progressed. It returned respectable earnings and made sensible investments in the development of Bentley and modernisation of its factory. The fresh management began to change Crewe's cloistered mindsets. Rolls-Royce began to understand that it could no longer operate in a vacuum, a genteel purveyor of motoring jewels to a wealthy and discerning clientele. It was part of an aggressive international industry, and had to act accordingly.

But new decades seemed to bring new crises at Rolls-Royce. The aerospace calamity of 1971 was followed by the successful rebuilding of consumer confidence in the cars, and the achievement of record sales at the end of the decade. The sudden sales famine of the early 1980s required another reconstruction, culminating in the near-record sales of 1990. The exercise was then repeated. The following years saw global demand for cars drop significantly. For Rolls-Royce and Bentley it plummeted. The company's sales collapsed from well over 3,000 in both 1989 and 1990 to just above 1,700 in 1991 and around 1,400 for each of the following three years. Neither was it a regional phenomenon that would permit a company to shift its business to the bright spots. Pockets of optimism were in very short supply.

In 1990, Iraq invaded Kuwait, which was later liberated by allied forces headed by the United States. Civil war developed in Yugoslavia. There was an attempted coup against President Mikhail Gorbachev in Russia. Japan's economic bubble burst. Latin America ran into a debt crisis. Germany was bogged down with the cost of unification after the Berlin Wall was demolished in November 1989. Share prices remained depressed as the effects of these and other events were felt around the world. And buyers stayed away from car showrooms.

Rolls-Royce Motor Cars had no option but to embark on another painful restructuring. The cost to the company was £50 million. The cost to the workforce was 2,500 jobs lost out of a total of around 5,500. Half the company's skill base was to be lost, a terrible waste of talent that could not be utilised elsewhere. They were dark days for Rolls-Royce, and for Crewe, where the run-down of the old railway engineering works was almost complete. The social implications for a small community were immense, as the lucky ones who still had jobs inevitably encountered their former colleagues in the streets, in the shops and in the pubs.

The brunt of the cuts was felt at Crewe, but also involved the relocation of the old Mulliner-Park Ward works in London to the headquarters site. The majority of the job losses were through voluntary redundancies, but around 500 people received compulsory notices. Surprisingly, while it was a tense time in Crewe, no time or days were lost on the factory floor through spontaneous protest. One director recalled: "When people who had been made redundant went to collect their papers and pay-offs at the end of the week, two directors were there to thank them. We didn't know what the reaction would be, whether they would try to hit us or cry on our shoulder. They did both."

The effect was to reduce Crewe's break-even point from 1,750 cars a year to 1,250, which meant by 1993 the company was trading profitably once more. Over the previous two years, though, it had lost money at a rate of around £1 million a week. As a large element of Vickers – at least a third, depending on the year – the performance also splashed a lot of red ink across the group. It was an experience that provoked Vickers into thinking about its exposure to the volatile world of the motor industry.

Looking to the longer term, it was clear Rolls-Royce would face the twin challenges of creeping competition and scale. In a world that buys 40 million new passenger cars a year, fewer than 2,000 of them were Rolls-Royces or Bentleys. To an automotive group with a sales turnover of $50 billion a year, the financial performance of a subsidiary the size of Rolls-Royce/Bentley – whether it made a small profit or a small loss – would barely matter. A big car group probably now spends more each year on IT systems than any Rolls-Royce or Bentley division could achieve in sales.

However, the public profiles, the reputations, of such companies are far higher than simple statistics suggest. The halo effect of a top-quality, globally recognised trophy brand within a group is immeasurable. Another simple reason why mass producers like prestigious brands is that they have the potential to produce a more interesting return on sales, which was why there was a broad push by the big groups into the higher end of the market. Many did so through acquisition.

Three Japanese firms tried with varying degrees of success to achieve the same result by creating new brands to attract wealthy customers in the United States. First, Honda established the separate Acura brand, then Nissan appeared with Infiniti and Toyota with Lexus. The reason was clear: the profit margin on a Lexus is much greater than on a Toyota Corolla. What all of this added up to was a chain of aspirant brands. The aim of the Lexus and Infiniti, Audi and Volvo, was to ape the social standing and profit margins of BMW and Mercedes-Benz, which in turn were pushing towards Rolls-Royce and Bentley. All were definitely succeeding on a technology level, and to an impressive extent in customer perception terms. While a Lexus today is still not regarded as an alternative to a Rolls-Royce, who knows what Lexus's standing in the market will be over two or three more generations of vehicles? Vickers, with Rolls-Royce and Bentley comfortably grazing in the sunniest part of the sales meadow, could hear the sound of a distant thunderstorm, and it was edging closer. The blast of consolidation elsewhere in the motor industry would have the effect of making the scale of Vickers' twin jewels more vulnerable.

The history of the motor industry is one of small companies being taken over by large groups. While the phenomenon is not new, the 1980s and 1990s were witness to some particularly grand strategic moves. Collectively, the number and scale of the changes redefined the shape of the international motor industry.

The Volkswagen group, later to feature so prominently in the destiny of Crewe, was particularly active. Under visionary chairman Ferdinand Piëch, Volkswagen consolidated its take-over of Seat in Spain and Skoda in the Czech Republic, and then bought Lamborghini and Bugatti in Italy before turning its attention to Bentley. The result, along with internal growth, was to double the scale of the group in less than a decade.

BMW, the present owner of Rolls-Royce, also went on the acquisition trail, though ultimately not as successfully. It dramatically bought the Rover group in 1994 and then just as rapidly dispensed with all of it except Mini six years later. Daimler-Benz, another company destined to play its part in the Rolls-Royce and Bentley drama, stunned the world by its acquisition (which the group insists was a merger) of Chrysler in the United States. DaimlerChrysler then all-but took over Mitsubishi Motors.

Elsewhere, the enormous shake-out during that period saw control of Aston Martin, Jaguar, Land Rover, Volvo and Mazda pass to Ford; Saab and Daewoo Motor to General Motors, which also bought strategic stakes in Fiat Auto, Isuzu, Suzuki and Fuji Heavy Industries (Subaru); Alfa Romeo and Maserati to Fiat; Kia Motors to Hyundai Motor; an alliance of Nissan with Renault, which bought controlling shares in Dacia in Romania and Samsung Motors in South Korea.

Similar upheaval took place in the industries involved in commercial vehicles and components. The only car makers to eschew the merger mania were Peugeot-Citroën, Porsche, Honda and Toyota. The overall result was that the big groups got bigger while the small ones were reduced in size or were swallowed up.

As we have seen, there was another important and parallel development. The diversified industrial groups that once embraced aerospace, heavy trucks, buses and much else besides, in addition to passenger cars, came collectively to the conclusion that specialisation was best. So when Vickers became disillusioned with its ownership of

Rolls-Royce and Bentley it became part of these seismic shifts. There was open speculation in the early 1990s that Vickers was looking for a buyer for Rolls-Royce. It was at the time, but in the end it elected to take a different course.

CHAPTER 13

BMW MAKES ITS MARK

Vickers really began to lose faith in Rolls-Royce when car sales plummeted in 1991. The group felt a particular responsibility to its shareholders who suffered throughout 1991-92 because of what was happening at Rolls-Royce. Vickers had to consider whether Rolls-Royce would be an appropriate part of its portfolio in the future. Sir David Plastow, the former head of Rolls-Royce who was by then chairman and chief executive of Vickers, decided to make some discrete inquiries among his friends in the motor industry. Nothing formal, all highly secret, just exploratory "What if?" questions.

Plastow went to Japan to meet a man he had come to know when he was president of the Society of Motor Manufacturers and Traders in the late 1970s. During that period senior members of the SMMT met their opposite numbers at the Japan Automobile Manufacturers' Association twice a year to discuss "prudent" export restraint to Britain on the part of Japan's vehicle makers. The man Plastow went to meet was Eiji Toyoda, chairman and scion of the family-controlled Toyota. While Toyota was Japan's biggest vehicle maker, it was not then the international powerhouse it is today. Could Rolls-Royce and Toyota find any mutually beneficial ways in which to do business? Just what the reaction would have been to any technical or financial alliance between a British national treasure and a presumptuous Japanese maker of family cars (which was how

Toyota was generally perceived in Europe at the time) can only be imagined. The world will never know, because a senior official of Toyota, a deeply cautious organisation, later told a press briefing in Osaka that it was not prepared to make the "quick decision" that Vickers sought.

There was much open speculation in late 1991 and early 1992 about possible buyers for Rolls-Royce. All the usual suspects were fair game for the media, but one group was consistently mentioned more than most: BMW. There were official denials all round, but Plastow and Sir Colin Chandler, the chief executive designate of Vickers, did discuss the topic in late 1991 with Dr Wolfgang Reitzle, the influential board member responsible for product engineering at BMW at the time.

When no concrete take-over offer emerged from BMW, or any other company, Vickers adopted a strategy that postponed the Rolls-Royce sale. However, unknown to Vickers, BMW was more interested in Rolls-Royce than it wanted to acknowledge. On a train journey across Japan towards the end of the 1980s, Reitzle and BMW chairman Eberhard v. Kuenheim chatted about the long term strategy for the group. BMW, they decided, needed to broaden the market appeal of its models. When the opportunities presented themselves, it should therefore buy Rolls-Royce and Land Rover, both of which made models outside BMW's traditional market categories. Neither was for sale at the time, but it started the process whereby BMW began to make its technology available to Rolls-Royce.

The train conversation also led BMW to begin the initial engineering and marketing studies for some type of sport-utility vehicle (one would appear as the X5 in 1999) and for a limousine referred to internally as the 9-series. One of the prime reasons why BMW subsequently bought the Rover group was to get its hands on Land Rover. While BMW sold Land Rover to Ford in 2000 – and Reitzle quit BMW – the much-admired Range Rover of 2002 is regarded as a legacy of Reitzle's reign at the company.

So, when Plastow and Chandler came courting, Reitzle was keen that his company should buy Rolls-Royce. His chairman was not.

Von Kuenheim, his thoughts shaped by the then-current debate about whether there was a future for large, luxury limousines, did not share the volume forecasts Vickers had for Rolls-Royce. As events turned out, he was probably right. The average annual sales number for Rolls-Royce and Bentley over the previous decade (the 1980s) was just under 2,700 units. In the decade about to unfold, the average was just over 1,700 a year. The difference was sufficiently large to conclude that a fundamental shift in buying patterns took place among the world's wealthiest consumers during an era of unprecedented wealth-creation. Curiously, none of this was sufficient to deter BMW, Volkswagen and Mercedes-Benz from cornering the ultimate prestige car sector a decade later through, respectively, Rolls-Royce, Bentley and Maybach.

There was, though, a much more significant reason why BMW did not bite when Vickers dangled Rolls-Royce before it in 1991, as Bernd Pischetsrieder later explained. "We would have had to do the restructuring that was needed," he said in early 2003. By then, Pischetsrieder was chairman of Volkswagen. In 1991, he was BMW's board member for manufacturing, which meant the task would have been his responsibility. The job needed doing, as the Rolls-Royce actions in 1991-92 underlined. But with Britain's tabloid newspapers still fighting the Second World War, it would have been a public relations disaster for a new German owner to sack half the workforce at the factory that made the engines that powered the planes that defeated the Luftwaffe invasion in September 1940.

With no one prepared to pay what Vickers thought Rolls-Royce was worth, whatever that was, they were on their own. The painful contraction at Crewe continued, and Rolls-Royce broke even in the first half of 1993. While the company was back on track, its structure and scale were altered beyond recognition. The decision it still had to make was precisely how to replace the model that had been its mainstay since 1980. Worse, after Rolls-Royce racked up losses of £110 million over the two previous years, Vickers was not prepared to allocate much money for the job.

If Rolls-Royce did not have time on its side, BMW did. It also had plenty of money, in spite of a 1992 commitment to invest an initial $300 million in its first car factory in the United States. Cleverly, what came out of the meetings with Vickers was a 1992 agreement to supply Rolls-Royce with the type of vehicle technology a customer would not notice. It took the form, for example, of using BMW engineering facilities to develop Rolls-Royce and Bentley electronics and to improve body stiffnesses. Just to make sure the world knew what was happening, Pischetsrieder, who became chairman in May 1993, authorised a press leak about the extent of the work. The agreement effectively locked Rolls-Royce into the orbit of BMW and its main suppliers. Importantly, it had the effect of locking out other car makers as well. BMW had in mind its great rival in Stuttgart, Mercedes-Benz. It did not at that stage anticipate the ownership challenge that eventually came from Volkswagen.

When a small Bentley convertible concept known as Java was unveiled at the 1994 Geneva motor show, it was no surprise to learn that it would have been based on the platform of the previous generation BMW 5-series. It provided Rolls-Royce with a great deal of favourable publicity, but it was, of course, a luxury the company could not afford. The idea did not go away entirely, but the priority was to replace the Silver Spirit and its Bentley derivatives. As it could not afford to develop a new driveline and a new body, the company had to make a choice. It elected to design and engineer a completely new body shell, which it planned to make itself rather than buy from an outside supplier, and to source powertrains from another manufacturer.

It was a doubly controversial decision. First, Rolls-Royce had always made its own engines. They were its heart and soul, dating back to the foundations of the company. Second, Rolls-Royce had never made its own bodies. Until the arrival of the Silver Shadow in 1965, it made chassis and drivetrains fitted with other firms' bodywork. After 1965, its unitary body/chassis units were sourced from Pressed Steel (later absorbed into Rover) in Oxford. What Rolls-Royce proposed was a very radical change.

Rolls-Royce enlisted the help of Mayflower, the engineering

contract group that works for a wide variety of clients in the motor industry. In late 1997, a move by Mayflower chief executive John Simpson would trigger the chain of events that led to Rolls-Royce being formally put up for sale by Vickers. For the moment, though, it was agreed that Mayflower's press shop in Coventry, the works formerly known as Motor Panels, would supply most of the large stamped parts for the new generation of Rolls-Royces and Bentleys. A large proportion would also come from Vickers' pressing operations in Newcastle-upon-Tyne. All of them would be assembled in a £40 million body shop to be built in the space that was occupied by engine assembly. While the building work was in progress, putting the engines together for the current models would be moved to the Wellingborough facility of Cosworth Engineering, which Vickers bought in the spring of 1990. It would, of course, be only a short-term contract, because the strategy for the new generation of models specified sourcing engines from another vehicle maker.

By that time, engineering director Mike Dunne, the man recruited to create the new generation of cars, had retired in the dark days of 1992. The project director for what became the Silver Seraph and Arnage was Tony Gott, an engineer who would feature prominently in events that unfolded over the following decade. Gott worked for TI and Lotus before joining Rolls-Royce in 1984. He joined the new model programme in January 1994, just as it was being defined, and later went on to head the whole company. The pieces of the jigsaw were falling into place. The one missing item was the engine.

Peter Ward, Rolls-Royce's chairman, began the search for what he called "the best deal". Several engines were considered, including a V12 by Ford and General Motors' Northstar V8. However, it quickly became apparent the run-off would be between BMW and Mercedes-Benz. Through 1994, Ward and his colleagues made a series of visits to Mercedes in Stuttgart and BMW in Munich. Both companies took the opportunity to show off their latest secret gadgets as well as to offer the V12 and V8 engines being sought for Rolls-Royce and Bentley respectively. The British team was more familiar with BMW, its facilities and personnel because of the low-key technology supply agreement made two years earlier. They knew BMW could do a good job. Later, after the deal had been signed, BMW tried to tempt Chandler and his colleagues with a high-performance model based on the 7-series and known internally as the Goldfish. It was no ordinary 7-series, but a development model equipped with a V16 engine – a V12 with four extra cylinders. Chandler was impressed, Pischetsrieder later confirmed, but was not prepared to pay for its use in Rolls-Royces. BMW's offer to buy a 20 per cent share in Rolls-Royce was also rejected by Vickers, because at some point in the future it wanted to sell the car maker in its entirety.

However, it quickly became clear to the Rolls-Royce people that Mercedes offered the better solutions. Helmut Werner, the chairman of Mercedes-Benz, said he would make available a new V8 engine – known internally as E113 – that the company had under development. Werner promised that the engine, suitably modified by Cosworth to distinguish it from later Mercedes versions, could make its world debut in a Bentley. It was an offer the British team found very attractive. In addition to supplying V12s for the Rolls-Royce, Mercedes expressed an interest in developing a car on the basis of Mercedes technology.

When Rolls-Royce engineers came to analyse the merits of the four engines in development vehicles, their findings agreed with the commercial judgment reached by their colleagues: Mercedes was the right choice. In particular, they were concerned about the lack of pulling power of BMW's 4.4-litre V8 at low engine speeds, even when equipped with twin turbochargers. They also recognised that it was noisier, heavier and thirstier than the Mercedes unit. With one dissenting voice, the board of Rolls-Royce believed the company should take the Mercedes-Benz route.

There was a major problem, however. It revolved around Sir Ralph Robins, the chairman of aircraft engine maker Rolls-Royce plc, which held sway over the use of the Rolls-Royce name. In 1992, Rolls-Royce plc formed a joint venture with BMW to design and develop a new generation of medium-sized airliner fan jets, the BR-

710. One of BMW's main rivals in that field was MTU, a company owned by Daimler-Benz, the parent group of Mercedes-Benz. Pischetsrieder, conscious of the way Rolls-Royce Motor Cars was leaning, made it his business to ensure Chandler was on message. He also made sure that Robins, his business partner in the aircraft engine deal, would help to persuade Chandler – a man whose career had been spent in the arms industry – of the wisdom of the BMW proposal as well.

The executive board of Vickers met to decide the issue in mid-December 1994 on the top floor of the Vickers tower on London's Millbank. The chairman, Sir Richard Lloyd, was not present so the meeting was chaired by Chandler, the chief executive. Andrew Johns, the commercial director, Roger Head, the finance director, and Peter Ward, the operations managing director, made up the quorum. Ward was concerned about the quiet lobbying that had taken place, but voted for what he and his fellow board members at Rolls-Royce thought best – Mercedes-Benz. When the other three plumped for BMW, Ward knew his days at Vickers were numbered.

A press conference in the theatre of the Vickers building a few days before Christmas ended months of speculation about whether the engine supplier would be Mercedes or BMW. It was attended by Pischetsrieder, Chandler and a clearly ill-at-ease Ward. Chandler said the decision was made on the basis of a more competitive deal from BMW. That would have been because of BMW's longer-term designs on Rolls-Royce itself. Chandler also reiterated that Rolls-Royce was not for sale "in the foreseeable future". In the event, Vickers put Rolls-Royce and Bentley on the market before customers were able to buy cars equipped with the engines he had just agreed to purchase.

The moment was a personal triumph for Pischetsrieder. Less than a year earlier, and shortly after taking over as BMW chairman, he led a sudden and dramatic purchase of Rover, Britain's last indigenous mass car manufacturer. With it came a bevy of names from the history of the British motor industry, including Land Rover, Mini and MG. While the take-over was ultimately a failure, and cost Pischetsrieder his job, the euphoria at the time made him the toast of

Above: MARQUE OF EXCELLENCE. CHARLES SYKES' SPIRIT OF ECSTASY RADIATOR STATUE
CAME TO EPITOMISE ROLLS-ROYCE'S "BEST CAR IN THE WORLD" EPITHET. IT CONTINUED TO SHINE
AFTER THE MARQUE SUBSEQUENTLY LOST ITS LUSTRE.

Above: AMBITIOUS YOUNG MAN. HENRY ROYCE HAD CREATED A THRIVING ELECTRICAL ENGINEERING AND CRANE BUSINESS BY THE TIME HIS FIRST CAR APPEARED IN 1904. THAT SAME YEAR, HE AGREED TO GO INTO BUSINESS WITH CHARLES ROLLS.

Above: Successful old man. Henry Royce at the wheel of a Silver Ghost outside his home in England at West Wittering, Sussex. The house is a few miles from the new Rolls-Royce factory at Goodwood.

Above: Man about town. The patriotic Charles Rolls – here at the wheel of a 1905 Rolls-Royce 20 HP – wanted to sell an English-made car rather than French imports at his London premises.

Above: Rolls-Royce moves downmarket. The cheaper, underpowered 20 HP launched in 1922 was regarded with disdain by traditional enthusiasts. In the austerity that followed the Wall Street crash, however, the series proved a saviour for the company.

Left: MOTORING PIONEERS. THE ORIGINAL SILVER GHOST HELPED TO ESTABLISH THE ROLLS-ROYCE REPUTATION IN THE 15,000 MILES RELIABILITY TRIAL OF 1907. AT THE WHEEL IS THE BUSINESSMAN REGARDED AS THE HYPHEN IN ROLLS-ROYCE – CLAUDE JOHNSON.

Below: ROLLS-ROYCE JOINS THE ARMY. ARMOURED VERSIONS OF THE SILVER GHOST SERVED THE BRITISH MILITARY WITH UTMOST RELIABILITY IN THE GREAT WAR. T.E. LAWRENCE – LAWRENCE OF ARABIA – FAMOUSLY DESCRIBED HIS GHOST AS MORE VALUABLE THAN RUBIES.

Above: THOSE WERE THE DAYS. WATNEY, KIDSTON, BARNATO AND CLEMENT CELEBRATE BENTLEY'S FIFTH LE MANS VICTORY IN 1930. THE FOLLOWING YEAR, BENTLEY WAS FORCED TO CALL IN THE RECEIVERS.

Above: IT'S A BENTLEY, BUT NOT AS BUYERS HAD KNOWN THEM. AFTER BUYING BENTLEY IN 1931, ROLLS-ROYCE MOVED THE COMPANY TO DERBY. THE BENTLEY $3^1/2$ LITRE OF 1934, A FINE CAR KNOWN AS THE "SILENT SPORTS CAR", WAS A ROLLS-ROYCE IN ALL BUT NAME.

Above: HERE TODAY, GONE TOMORROW. W.O. BENTLEY CREATED HIS OWN CAR COMPANY AFTER THE GREAT WAR IN SPITE OF ENORMOUS DIFFICULTIES. WITHIN A DECADE, THOUGH, BENTLEY MOTORS HAD BEEN BOUGHT BY ROLLS-ROYCE. W.O. WAS TREATED SHABBILY BY THE NEW OWNERS.

Above: HIGH SOCIETY. THIS 1936 PHANTOM III WITH BODYWORK BY THRUPP & MABBERLY WAS ORIGINALLY BUILT FOR COUNT HAUGWITZ REVENTLOW. HIS SON, LANCE, WOULD LATER FUND THE CREATION OF SCARAB RACING CARS.

Left: ROLLS-ROYCE PRIORITIES CHANGED IN 1939, AS THE COMPANY TRANSFERRED ALL OUTPUT TO ENGINES LIKE THE MERLIN IN THIS SPITFIRE. CREWE, THE POST-WAR HOME OF THE CAR BUSINESS, WAS ESTABLISHED SPECIFICALLY TO MAKE AIRCRAFT ENGINES.

Bottom left: PHANTOM ILLUSION. WHEN HENRY ROYCE SET OUT TO BUILD A CAR WITHOUT ENGINEERING AND FINANCIAL COMPROMISE, HE CREATED THE PHANTOM OF 1925. THIS IS A SERIES II OF 1931 WITH BODYWORK BY CARLTON. AFTER THE CO-FOUNDER DIED, THE COMPANY ADOPTED A MORE REALISTIC PRODUCT POLICY.

Below: THE POWER AND THE GLORY. THE WARTIME ACHIEVEMENTS OF THE MERLIN AIRCRAFT ENGINE – IT WAS USED IN THE SPITFIRE, HURRICANE, LANCASTER, MOSQUITO AND MUSTANG AMONG MANY OTHERS – LAID THE FOUNDATIONS OF ROLLS-ROYCE'S POST-WAR SUCCESS IN AVIATION. UNFORTUNATELY, THAT SUCCESS BLINDED THE COMPANY TO THE POSSIBILITY OF FAILURE.

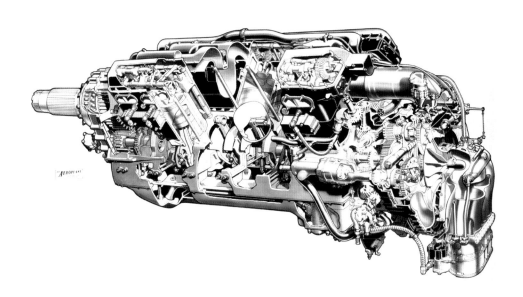

Left: The shape of things to come. For those with money, nothing was more chic in the early 1950s than the Bentley Continental R – the fastest four-seater in the world. It was a grand gesture in the drab post-war era of austerity and rationing in Britain.

Above: Ah, yes. The first proper post-war Rolls-Royce was the S1 Silver Cloud launched in 1955. John Blatchley's classic design stood the test of time so well it influenced BMW designers when they came to create the 2003 Phantom.

Above: You're the tops. Silver Shadows like this Series II became the most popular Rolls-Royces of all time. The original car, launched in 1965, was the first Rolls-Royce to use unitary construction. Unfortunately, its long period in production came just as new technology was beginning to sweep through the rest of the car industry.

Above: TURBULENT TIMES. DAVID PLASTOW HAD BEEN MANAGING DIRECTOR OF ROLLS-ROYCE'S CAR DIVISION FOR ONLY A MONTH WHEN THE PARENT COMPANY COLLAPSED IN FEBRUARY 1971 BECAUSE OF THE RB-211 AERO ENGINE CONTRACT. HE LED THE CAR COMPANY TO A STOCK EXCHANGE LISTING AND THE SUBSEQUENT MERGER WITH VICKERS.

Above: ROYAL APPROVAL. UNLIKE HER FATHER AND GRANDFATHER, WHO PREFERRED DAIMLERS, FOR STATE OCCASIONS QUEEN ELIZABETH II FAVOURED ROLLS-ROYCES, LIKE THIS PHANTOM V SEEN IN THE EARLY 1970S. HOWEVER, TO MARK HER GOLDEN JUBILEE, THE QUEEN WAS GIVEN A COACHBUILT BENTLEY BY BRITAIN'S CAR INDUSTRY IN 2002.

Above: OTHER-WORLDLY. THIS FINE HOUSE IN THE SOUTH OF FRANCE IS LE CANADEL, HENRY ROYCE'S HOME. ROYCE'S HEALTH DICTATED HE SPENT SUMMERS IN SUSSEX AND WINTERS IN FRANCE. HE BARELY VISITED THE COMPANY'S HEADQUARTERS IN LONDON OR THE FACTORY IN DERBY, AND YET EVERY PRODUCT DECISION REVOLVED AROUND THE CO-FOUNDER.

Left: SIR DENNING PEARSON, THE CHIEF EXECUTIVE, WAS ADMONISHED IN THE OFFICIAL GOVERNMENT REPORT INTO THE COLLAPSE OF ROLLS-ROYCE. THE REPORT'S AUTHORS CAME TO THE CONCLUSION: "THEY (PEARSON AND SIR DAVID HUDDIE, MANAGING DIRECTOR OF THE AERO ENGINE DIVISION) FAILED TO DISCHARGE THE RESPONSIBILITIES OF STEWARDSHIP WHICH REST UPON DIRECTORS OF PUBLIC COMPANIES."

Above: OH, DEAR. PININFARINA'S CAMARGUE OF 1975, BASED ON THE SILVER SHADOW, WAS NOT A PICTURE OF ELEGANCE. HOWEVER, IT SERVED ROLLS-ROYCE EXCEPTIONALLY WELL AT A CRITICAL TIME BY SEPARATING WEALTHY BUYERS FROM LOTS OF THEIR MONEY.

Previous Page: GRAND ILLUSION. THE SWISH ROLLS-ROYCE CORNICHE LOOKED THE PART DURING THE ALMOST QUARTER OF A CENTURY OF ITS EXISTENCE. BUT IT WAS DURING THIS PERIOD THAT THE COMPANY SLIPPED BEHIND MERCEDES-BENZ AND BMW IN TERMS OF QUALITY, RELIABILITY AND TECHNOLOGY.

Above: STEPPING DOWN. THE SILVER SPIRIT SERIES, WHICH LATER INCLUDED THIS LONG WHEELBASE SILVER SPUR DERIVATIVE, APPEARED IN 1980 AND CONTINUED IN PRODUCTION FOR 18 YEARS. THE RANGE NEVER ACHIEVED THE SALES SUCCESS OF ITS PREDECESSORS, IN SPITE OF THE BENTLEY REVIVAL.

Above: DOING THE CONTINENTAL. AFTER ROLLS-ROYCE RE-AWOKE TO THE SALES POTENTIAL OF THE BENTLEY MARQUE, IT PRODUCED THE CONTINENTAL R IN 1991. THE NAME WAS AN UNASHAMED COPY OF THE FAMOUS MODEL OF THE 1950S.

Left: BENTLEY BOY. PETER WARD, WHO WENT ON TO BECAME CHIEF EXECUTIVE, WAS PART OF A YOUNGER TEAM BROUGHT INTO ROLLS-ROYCE IN THE EARLY 1980S. HE IMMEDIATELY IDENTIFIED THE NEGLECTED MARKET POTENTIAL OF THE BENTLEY BRAND, BUT QUIT WHEN VICKERS OVERRULED HIS PREFERRED ENGINE STRATEGY.

Right: SUPER-SALESMAN. SIR COLIN CHANDLER HAD ALREADY ACHIEVED GREAT SUCCESS IN THE ARMS BUSINESS BEFORE BECOMING VICKERS CHAIRMAN. HIS BREAK-UP OF THE FAMOUS OLD ENGINEERING GROUP, INCLUDING THE SALE OF ROLLS-ROYCE MOTOR CARS, RESULTED IN HANDSOME REWARDS FOR VICKERS SHAREHOLDERS.

Above: HAPPIER DAYS. ROLLS-ROYCE CHIEF EXECUTIVE GRAHAM MORRIS WAS ON HOLIDAY WHEN HE LEARNED VICKERS WAS SELLING HIS COMPANY. HE LATER RESIGNED BECAUSE OF THE DECISION TO SPLIT ROLLS-ROYCE AND BENTLEY.

Above: GOTT THE JOB. TONY GOTT INITIALLY BECAME CHIEF EXECUTIVE OF ROLLS-ROYCE AND BENTLEY DURING THE VOLKSWAGEN TRANSITION PERIOD AFTER GRAHAM MORRIS LEFT. HE THEN ABRUPTLY SWITCHED TO BMW'S PROJECT ROLLS-ROYCE.

Above: DONE DEAL. THE WORLD LEARNED WHAT WAS TO BECOME OF ROLLS-ROYCE AND BENTLEY AT A PRESS BRIEFING IN LONDON ON JULY 28, 1998. A DEAL WAS QUIETLY STITCHED TOGETHER BY SIR RALPH ROBINS (LEFT), CHAIRMAN OF ROLLS-ROYCE PLC, AND BERND PISCHETSRIEDER (CENTRE), CHAIRMAN OF BMW. VOLKSWAGEN CHAIRMAN FERDINAND PIËCH (RIGHT) KNEW THE SCORE BECAUSE HE AND PISCHETSRIEDER HELD SECRET MEETINGS TO DISCUSS THE DIVISION OF BRITAIN'S AUTOMOTIVE CROWN JEWELS.

Bentley is back. Immediately after buying Bentley, Volkswagen decided the marque had to return to Le Mans, where it pulled off a convincing one-two in 2003 – its first win there for 73 years. *Above:* The Speed 8 of Guy Smith/Dindo Capello/Tom Kristensen was fastest qualifier in 2003. *Right:* The chequered flag is raised as Bentley conquers Le Mans once again.

Above: HERE'S ONE I BOUGHT EARLIER. BERND PISCHETSRIEDER LED BMW'S PURCHASE OF THE ROVER GROUP IN 1994 A FEW MONTHS AFTER BECOMING CHAIRMAN. FOUR YEARS LATER HE BOUGHT ROLLS-ROYCE FOR BMW. AND SHORTLY AFTER THAT, BMW DISPENSED WITH THE SERVICES OF PISCHETSRIEDER AND ROVER.

Above: IN AT THE DEEP END. CHRIS WOODWARK, THE COSWORTH ENGINEERING CHAIRMAN, WAS GIVEN ADDED RESPONSIBILITY FOR ROLLS-ROYCE WHEN PETER WARD SUDDENLY QUIT AS CHIEF EXECUTIVE. WOODWARK TOOK TOUGH COST-CUTTING DECISIONS WHILE OVERSEEING DEVELOPMENT OF THE NEW GENERATION SILVER SERAPH AND ARNAGE.

Next page: THE WAY FORWARD. THE VOLKSWAGEN PURCHASE ALLOWED BENTLEY TO INVEST IN THE DEVELOPMENT OF A NEW GENERATION OF CARS. THE CONTINENTAL GT OF 2003 CAPTURES THE SPIRIT OF BENTLEYS PAST. OTHER DERIVATIVES ARE PLANNED.

Above: HAPPINESS IS BENTLEY. FERDINAND PIËCH, CHAIRMAN OF VOLKSWAGEN, MAINTAINED ALL ALONG THAT HE ONLY EVER WANTED TO BUY BENTLEY, NOT ROLLS-ROYCE. WHEN PIËCH RETIRED, FORMER BMW MAN PISCHETSRIEDER REPLACED HIM AT VOLKSWAGEN.

Left: ANGLO-GERMAN ENTERPRISE. MODERN ROLLS-ROYCES UNDER BMW OWNERSHIP ARE ASSEMBLED IN A HIGH-TECH, ECO-FRIENDLY FACTORY JUST OUTSIDE CHICHESTER, ENGLAND. DESPITE THE CAR'S TRADITIONAL NAME, THOUGH, VIRTUALLY NONE OF ITS CONTENT IS SOURCED IN BRITAIN.

Bottom left: LAST OF THE LINE. THE ARNAGE WAS THE LAST BENTLEY DEVELOPED IN AN INDEPENDENT COMPANY UNDER VICKERS. BENTLEY'S FUTURE WILL MEAN GREATER COMPONENT-SHARING WITH VOLKSWAGEN GROUP COMPANIES.

Below: ANYTHING YOU CAN DO... MERCEDES-BENZ TOOK A VERY CLOSE LOOK WHEN VICKERS PUT ROLLS-ROYCE MOTOR CARS UP FOR SALE. IN THE END, MERCEDES ELECTED TO PRODUCE A ROLLS-ROYCE RIVAL OF ITS OWN – THE MAYBACH.

Above: THE BEST CAR IN THE WORLD? BMW'S AMBITION IS TO MAKE ROLLS-ROYCE WORTHY OF ITS OLD EPITHET ONCE MORE. ITS STARTING POINT WAS THE GIANT PHANTOM, A TRADITIONAL NAME FOR A THOROUGHLY MODERN LIMOUSINE.

the British motor industry. Securing the Rolls-Royce engine agreement only confirmed his stature.

For Pischetsrieder to reach that point, though, required Vickers to ignore the advice of the motor industry experts it employed. What might, outside the arms and aerospace industry, have been an uncomplicated automotive decision was defeated by behind-the-scenes Anglo-German power politicking by Robins and Pischetsrieder. They were destined to play the same double act to secure the ownership of Rolls-Royce Motor Cars for BMW three and a half years later.

Ward resigned a few days after the decision, but agreed to stay until April to help with the transition. The following month, he was named chairman and chief executive of Cunard, the luxury shipping and cruise line owned by Trafalgar House, based in New York. Immediately after Ward quit, Chandler phoned the Farnham Common home of Chris Woodwark, a former Rover executive recruited the previous year to run Vickers' Cosworth operation. Suddenly, Woodwark found himself chief executive of Rolls-Royce, which carried membership of the Vickers board, as well as chairman of Cosworth.

Vickers' choice of engine supplier that December was something of a preliminary skirmish. The real battle would not take place until nearly four years later. But the decision had a number of implications for the people and companies involved. In addition to the departure of Ward, the failure of Mercedes' Werner to secure the high profile Rolls-Royce contract in competition with the upstarts from Munich represented a loss of face. Werner was already on wobbly ground because of his opposition to the plan by the Daimler-Benz chairman, Juergen Shrempp, to fold Mercedes into the group structure – and thus eliminate Werner's role. When he finally quit in January 1997, Werner practically became a non-person at the German automaker, in spite of launching a visionary strategy to broaden the Mercedes range with the A-class, M-class, V-class and other models.

Primarily, though, the decision would provide BMW with the

inside track to secure the ownership of Rolls-Royce whenever Vickers decided the time was right. BMW made the most of the advantage. Rolls-Royce did not have the in-house capacity or capability to develop many of the features of the new models such as the air conditioning, electronic management and suspension systems. Ever-obliging, kindly BMW helped out, safe in the knowledge that every time it did so, Rolls-Royce and Bentley took on a more distinct BMW flavour. That was the cornerstone of Pischetsrieder's strategy: to make Rolls-Royce and Bentley so dependent on BMW technology that it would cost another company a fortune in time and money to take it out.

That, of course, was precisely what happened when Volkswagen secured Bentley. The original Arnage was such a failure in the market place, as the company privately predicted it would be when equipped with the inadequate BMW V8, that Volkswagen's first action was to take the traditional 6.75-litre pushrod V8 out of mothballs. The crash programme to make it comply with forthcoming emissions regulations is said to have cost a fortune, but it gave the Arnage the push it needed, both dynamically and in the market place.

However, while the very public tug-of-war over engines was taking place between BMW and Mercedes, Rolls-Royce had quietly developed a very powerful new ally of a different type. It was a car addict who was so acquisitive and so wealthy that his purchases during the mid-1990s enabled Rolls-Royce to fund the Silver Seraph and Arnage development programmes, and return a handsome profit to Vickers. The client insisted on absolute confidentiality, but, with the passage of time, a picture has emerged of the man who amassed the world's largest car collection. The role he played in Rolls-Royce's fortunes at that time is astonishing.

CHAPTER 14

THE BRUNEI BONANZA

Peter Ward was at the preview to the Geneva motor show in March 1991 savouring a moment of good news. The previous year had been excellent for Rolls-Royce and the revived Bentley marque, but the first indications were coming in of what was to be a fearsome economic recession. Ward knew what the implications would be for Rolls-Royce and its workforce at Crewe. In Geneva, though, he had just unveiled the prototype of the Bentley Continental R, the first dedicated Bentley product since the 1950s. The reception had been terrific. Ward knew the company would have a winner when production of the Continental began the following year.

On the company's show stand, he chatted with a representative of the Brunei royal family. As the Sultan of Brunei was generally acknowledged to be the world's richest man at the time, Ward paid close attention. Rolls-Royce had supplied a number of cars to the Brunei royal family, including several six-door limousines in the 1980s, and orders kept trickling in over the years. The buying stakes were about to be raised to levels no one in the world had previously experienced.

"My client wishes to buy the Continental R," the Brunei representative told Ward.

"You don't understand. The car is only a prototype," Ward told him.

"No, *you* don't understand. My client *really* wishes to buy this car."

So began the extraordinary saga of how Prince Jefri and his eldest son, Prince Hakeem, underwrote the Rolls-Royce car business in a quest to build the greatest private car collection the world has known. The princes got their Continental, of course. Over the next few years, they complemented it with 22 more. These, though, they specified should include some Continental four-door estate cars. They were indicative of the men's tastes and the scale of their funds.

The cliché about life imitating art was never more apt. The Brunei royals seemed almost like real-life replicas of the Eddie Murphy character in *Coming to America*. The central character of the 1988 movie was an immensely wealthy African prince with feudal ideas and unlimited funds let loose in the United States. By coincidence, Murphy's fictional pampered prince was called Akeem.

Brunei is a tiny country not much larger than Norfolk with a population of about 330,000. With a history stretching back 1,000 years, Brunei was formerly a British colony and only became fully independent in 1984. Its phenomenal wealth stems from oil and natural gas. The people are mainly ethnic Malay, predominantly Muslim, but there is also a significant minority of Chinese origin. Located on the island of Borneo, Brunei is wedged between the Malaysian states of Sarawak and Sabah. Government departments employ 75 per cent of the working population, who pay no tax and enjoy free education and health care. In this most generous of welfare states no one is poor, but some are definitely wealthier than others.

Sultan Hassanal Bolkiah, trained at the British military academy at Sandhurst, rules this tiny realm from a gold-domed palace built on the edge of the Borneo jungle. The palace is on the scale of Versailles and is said to contain over 1,700 rooms and a banqueting hall that can seat 5,000. As a younger man, Sultan Hassanal knew how to have a good time, but more recently, mindful of his obligations and aware of the rise of Muslim fundamentalism in the region, has led a less flamboyant life. There were no such constraints on his younger brother, Prince Jefri, during the early part of the 1990s.

The sultan, who also acts as prime minister and defence minister, made Jefri the country's finance minister and the head of the secretive Brunei Investment Agency. The agency was established to invest the country's enormous financial reserves said to be worth in total over $100 billion. It may not have been the shrewdest appointment ever made by a prime minister. Jefri also owned his own conglomerate, Amedeo Development Corporation. There were times when the prince clearly found it difficult to differentiate between BIA and Amedeo. When Amedeo – named after the Italian artist Amedeo Modigliani – collapsed in 1998 in the wake of the Asian economic crisis, it had debts of $3.5 billion.

And when Hassanal sued Jefri and 75 of his hangers-on in 2000 for "improper withdrawal and use" of $40 billion state funds in order to prop up Amedeo, some idea of Jefri's lifestyle began to filter out. Court documents revealed Jefri – apparently known as P.J. among his advisers – had a daily spending habit of $747,000 over a 10-year period. He bought the Plaza Athenee hotel in Paris, the Palace hotel in New York, the former Playboy Club in London and Asprey & Garrard, the London jewellers, where he was the firm's best customer. If Jefri bought an Airbus airliner, Hakeem decided he needed one as well. Jefri's most famous purchase was a 46-metre yacht which he named *Tits*. The boat's two tenders were, surprise, surprise, called *Nipple I* and *Nipple II*. And, of course, a man with four wives, 35 children and 2,000 polo ponies to support clearly needed plenty of spending money.

The sultan and his brother eventually settled the dispute out of court and an order was made for a collection of Jefri's awesome trinkets to be auctioned to repay some of the debt. The sale, organised by British auctioneers Smith Hodgkinson, took place in Bandar Seri Begawan, the capital, in August 2001. It took six days for the auctioneers to dispose of the contents of 21 warehouses crammed with the treasures bought by Jefri during his years of excess.

The items that went under the hammer ranged from the bizarre to the exquisite. What they had in common was that they were all extremely expensive. They included multi-million dollar simulators for an Airbus A340, a Comanche attack helicopter and a Formula

One racing car. They included gold-plated lavatory brushes and 16,000 tonnes of Italian marble – enough to build another palace. There were 400 Victorian lamp standards, a couple of unused Mercedes-Benz fire appliances, a bronze rocking horse over 3 metres tall and several hundred Louis XIV-style chairs.

What was not auctioned was the stunning collection of cars collected in the 1990s by the playboy prince. In this mission, Jefri was encouraged by Prince Hakeem, a sports-mad, slightly overweight young man then in his early twenties. Estimates of the size of the collection range from 2,000 to 5,000 vehicles, most of which were kept in four air-conditioned, two-storey warehouses in the grounds of a Brunei palace.

Just as the 19th century's newly created railway and industrial barons in the United States scoured the old world for artworks and other treasures to decorate their own palaces back home, so Jefri's and Hakeem's representatives scooped up the best cars from Europe's best manufacturers. The big difference was that, unlike the 19th-century Americans, they appeared to be interested only in the present, not the past. Thus, examples of classic cars from history such as Bugattis, Duesenbergs or Hispano-Suizas were given scant attention. Jefri and Hakeem wanted their cars to be modern, fast and unique, which meant regular Ferraris barely passed muster. They had to be versions that no one else could buy. Money was not an issue.

The exact details of the collection are vague, because the Brunei royal family is not in the habit of inviting *Hello!* magazine into its palaces for happy snaps of smiling princes. It insists on privacy, and employs Ghurka troops to ensure its protection. In addition, while the legal dispute with his brother was settled out of court, hundreds of Jefri's other creditors are still owed money. It seems prudent to keep a lower profile.

The companies that supplied the cars in the first place are not prepared to discuss their clients' purchases. At this end of the car market, they never do unless a dispensation is issued by the buyer. The manufacturers take the long view. Prince Jefri may have stepped back from the exotic car market when his financial problems blew up, and the settlement with his brother reduced him to an allowance of only $300,000 a month, but his obsession with cars has not evaporated. Some time in the future, the circumstances may change. Car makers will be keen to pick up where they left off with their former customer.

However, there are enough anecdotes from people involved in the creation, transport and maintenance of these cars to build an overall picture of the shape and scale of the Jefri collection. There were plenty of standard production Ferraris, Lamborghinis, Aston Martins and Porsches, but they were almost beneath contempt. There were even rarer exotica like several McLaren F1s and Jaguar XJR-15s, but a Mercedes-Benz was not worth having unless it was tuned by Brabus or AMG. There was, however, at least one acknowledgement of the past when the princes ordered half a dozen 6-litre AMG-powered Mercedes 500SLs with special bodywork that made them look like the classic 300SLs of the 1950s. One source says little Aston Martin sold cars worth 15m-pounds to Jefri one year, equivalent to around a fifth of the firm's sales income around that time.

However, to set the princes' pulses racing, appearance, rarity and performance were paramount. Their cars had to have special bodies built to their approval or be fitted with more powerful engines, or both. They bought fully working versions of cars the world only knew as concept cars, such as the Ferrari Mythos from Pininfarina and the Bentley Java. Interestingly, in view of the subsequent ownership change at Rolls-Royce, it is understood no BMWs are in the collection.

For the car makers involved, meeting emissions, noise and crash-testing regulations were not issues. The completed cars were air-freighted in secure containers to Schipol airport in the Netherlands, where Brunei aircraft then flew them to their final destination. Once in Brunei, the royal family sets the rules and owns the roads, what few there are.

Autocar magazine in Britain published an eight-page illustrated feature about the Brunei cars in September 1998. Among the cars pictured were versions of the Ferrari 456 as four-door estate car and convertible, a Pininfarina-bodied Aston Martin Vantage and road-going editions of Dauer's Le Mans Porsche 962. The publication wrote about the secret collection's even more secret section where, it reported, every Formula One Championship-winning car since 1980 was displayed.

Jefri's fast car fetish was just bubbling up when his representative met Ward at that 1991 Geneva motor show. Unknowingly, the meeting was to provide a lifeline for Rolls-Royce and Bentley at a critical period in their history. Ward cultivated the Brunei connection as Crewe went through the painful restructuring of 1991-92. When Rolls-Royce's financial performance began to improve, the most pressing problem it faced was how to replace the range of Rolls-Royces and Bentleys it had sold since 1980. Vickers' controversial selection in 1994 of BMW over Mercedes-Benz as an engine supplier set the pattern for the future, but led to the departure of Ward as Rolls-Royce chief executive.

His replacement, Chris Woodwark, inherited the Brunei orders just as their engineering development gathered pace. He was not as close as Ward was to Hakeem, Jefri's main go-between, but custom-built Bentleys remained very popular in Brunei. So much so that, in spite of having to pay for the development of the new generation cars (the 1998 Silver Spirit and Arnage), and achieving only half the annual sales of 1990, Rolls-Royce did very well in the mid-1990s.

Brunei made the difference. The company broke even on its regular sales in 1993, and then began to make good money because of the Brunei specials. It achieved a return on sales of over 10 per cent, an unheard-of figure in an industry that is happy to get 5 per cent and only dreams about 10 per cent. The company delivered roughly 70 to 75 cars a year – mostly Bentleys and most of them turbocharged – to Brunei for the three years 1994-96 and into 1997. But they were not standard production cars. They were bespoke Bentleys costing Brunei up to £150 million a year. In other words, roughly half of the sales income at Rolls-Royce Motor Cars over a three-year period was attributable to a pair of stupendously wealthy Brunei princes.

Neither were they single car orders. Jefri and Hakeem initially commissioned two or three cars at a time, but when informed that higher volumes would mean lower unit prices, they bought each model by the half-dozen. The vehicles included the Dominator, which combined a unique body shape, Range Rover four-wheel-drive system and turbocharged Bentley engine. The cost was around £1.5 million each. They included half a dozen stretched Rolls-Royce Phantom VIs measuring 6.7 metres in length. The cars, which were built under contract by Pininfarina in Italy, were finished in dark blue and featured hand-beaten brass bumpers. They cost £6 million each. There was a whole raft of other specials, coupés and convertibles.

The Bentley Java concept car, originally displayed as a glassfibre mock-up without an opening bonnet and with no mechanical components, became a particular favourite. When Jefri expressed an interest, Cosworth, Bentley's sister company, quickly constructed a wooden engine to illustrate how the installation would look. The prince was convinced and ordered half a dozen each of the coupé, convertible and estate car versions. The cost was £750,000 apiece. One source says the Java's engine was actually a twin-turbo version of the BMW V8 from which all traces of the maker's name were eliminated because of the Brunei disdain for BMWs – a disdain that had its origins in a dispute about a BMW gearbox failure. Separately, Rolls-Royce used the Java as a starting point for an ultimately still-born production car programme that was known as MSB, or Medium-Sized Bentley.

The people at Bentley came to know the type of vehicle Jefri and Hakeem would go for. To secure an order, the company compiled beautiful, leather-bound books printed on the finest quality paper. They were pieces of artwork in themselves, the sort of books that would not be out of place on the coffee table in comfortable country homes. Other companies were known to produce video presentations about the cars they thought would interest the Brunei princes. Bentley's sales books contained the proposed specification for a car and were illustrated with colour renderings by artists or computer-generated images. The vehicles, of course, did not exist at that stage. It was the sort of elaborate promotion material that an architectural practice might compile for a major building it wanted to design.

Having received the order, Bentley then had to design, engineer and build the cars from scratch. In the case of the original Java concept, it was nothing more than a glassfibre shell. The project went through the same type of product development programme as a car destined for regular production car, except the final vehicle was costed over a handful of cars rather than hundreds or thousands. Development testing was done in secret at night at the Bruntingthorpe test track in England's East Midlands.

The Java and other orders were handled by a dedicated group of around 100 designers and engineers known as the Blackpool team. They worked within the Mulliner-Park Ward special customer department at Crewe under Jim Orr. However, not all of the cars were made there. The business was very attractive in the short term, but Rolls-Royce was not prepared to gear up with the additional overheads for mini-production runs when the bonanza might not exist in a few years' time. It proved a prescient decision. So, while the Brunei cars were designed and developed by the Blackpool team, construction of many of them was contracted out to a variety of top coach-building specialists, including Mayflower in Britain, Pininfarina in Italy and Hess & Eisenhardt in the United States before being returned to Mulliner-Park Ward for final validation.

The business proved very profitable and provided good cash flow. One potentially worrying aspect, though, was that there was no such thing as a written order for any of the cars destined for Brunei. The commissions, which were placed through one of Jefri's trading companies in London called Goldcrest, were conducted on a gentlemanly nod and wink basis. When Bentley's development spending rose to worrying levels, a request for additional funds was despatched to Goldcrest. The money was always forwarded promptly – at least in the early stages.

But when Jefri's lavish world began to collapse towards the end of 1997, several of the prince's favourite suppliers found themselves seriously exposed. They included Bentley, where Jefri had by that stage built up a sizeable debt. In pursuit of settlement, one former senior executive of the company recalls being taken to an anonymous office in London's Mayfair district and asked to wait. He was eventually handed a cheque for £6 million, the correct amount, by a person he had never seen before, or has or since.

When news broke in the autumn of 1997 that Vickers proposed to dispose of Rolls-Royce and Bentley, Jefri's agents were alarmed. They did not want their favourite car supplier to fall into the hands of any company they did not trust. Besides, Jefri's car collection indicated how dismissive he was of BMW products. Ownership by Volkswagen must have been an even more distasteful prospect for the world's greatest car snobs. A delegation representing the princes visited Crewe to decide whether to bid. In the end, they did not, and were certainly discouraged to do so by Rolls-Royce and Vickers. It is not clear why Jefri and his family stepped back from making an offer, but it may have been a reflection of the gathering economic storm in Asia and falling energy prices. Had they offered a large enough cheque, Vickers would have had to take the proposal seriously.

When Jefri's world fell apart in the wake of the Asian economic crisis and the failure of Amedeo, the Brunei fast car frenzy was over, for Bentley and every other beneficiary of his and Hakeem's largesse. Even today, car company executives shake their heads in disbelief at memories of the episode. It was a truly bizarre period. During the mid-1990s, the Brunei royal family's car-lust underwrote the Rolls-Royce and Bentley business plan, yet there was never anything in writing to confirm the orders. At the same time, the business allowed Rolls-Royce and Bentley to contribute half the profits to the parent Vickers group. In other words, the foundations of a respectable public group, which was also a prime defence contractor, were dependent on the whims of wealthy princes with insatiable appetites for cars. As it turned out, Vickers had another reason to be grateful for the Brunei business. There seems little doubt that, but for the unexpected cash bonus, BMW and Volkswagen would not have been prepared to offer quite as much as they did when Rolls-Royce Motor Cars was put up for sale.

CHAPTER 15

CREWE CHANGE

C hris Woodwark remembers an "appalling atmosphere" at Crewe when he arrived as chief executive at the end of 1994 to replace Peter Ward. It was quite a change from his previous place of work. Woodwark, a motor industry veteran from the Rover group, was recruited to run Cosworth Engineering in September 1993, the year Nigel Mansell won the CART Championship in North America in a Cosworth-powered Lola. The following year, Michael Schumacher won his first Formula One World Championship in a Cosworth-powered Benetton. But Cosworth was not just involved in the glamorous world of motor sport. It was a serious contractor to the general motor industry through engine development, engine assembly and advanced aluminium alloy castings. Then, literally overnight, Woodwark found himself presented with a much bigger challenge – as well as running Cosworth.

While he was largely unfamiliar with Rolls-Royce, equally no one at Crewe knew Woodwark. Rolls-Royce employees, who had lived through all the rumours about the sale of the company at the end of the 1980s and the dramatic retrenchment of 1991-92, had just seen one boss quit. Here was another destined to complicate their lives. At the time, Rolls-Royce engine builders were about to lose their jobs because of the scheme to move the assembly task to Cosworth. No one there knew anything about the disciplines of the body building they were about to undertake in order to construct the new generation of cars planned for 1998. The prospect of a company with its roots in engine manufacture becoming reliant on BMW for engines just added to the atmosphere of uncertainty and doubt at Crewe.

The site was also pretty run-down. Annual production had fallen well below the levels achieved in the latter part of the previous decade, and quality had slipped. This was annoying for customers and damaging to the firm's reputation, while carrying out repairs incurred additional warranty costs. The priorities were to modernise the production facilities, improve quality, and restore the battered morale of the people who worked at Crewe. At the same time Rolls-Royce had to develop an all-new range and, almost as an adjunct, satisfy the car cravings of the Brunei royal family.

Tony Gott, who went on to become chief executive at Crewe, worked in the engineering department at the time. "I don't recall many high points," he reported in early 2003. "Crewe was not an easy place to work in at that time. We were all determined to succeed, but the question was how. We needed help in engineering and investment."

When engine assembly was moved to Cosworth, the block in which it had been located was turned into the new body assembly area. Factory buildings were re-roofed and an effort was made to refurbish the plant after years of neglect. Installing the powered moving assembly track – a first for Rolls-Royce – then exposed a couple of underground streams. The company also installed a rolling road and shake test rig so that almost all the testing could be done in-house rather then on the open road in all weathers. The paint plant was refurbished to a water-based system saving 15 tonnes of solvent emissions a year. Money, always scarce, was invested in the wood and leather shops. A just-in-time parts delivery system was developed and, with the reduced volumes, the size of the stores could be reduced.

As part of an attempt to rebuild relations with employees, the company began to emphasise Crewe's role as a "centre of excellence" once more. Historically, it always was, but the ideal took a hammering through the traumas involving Rolls-Royce itself and the town in general because of the railway rundown. About 300 employees went through a retraining programme to learn how to make modern, unitary construction car bodies. In another first, in January 1996 Rolls-Royce appointed its first female board member when Christine Gaskell became head of the personnel department.

Two more controversial cost-saving decisions were taken in 1995-96. The offices and showroom in Conduit Street, the Mayfair premises dating back to the foundations of Rolls-Royce, were sold. As a pure showroom, with no direct sales function, Conduit Street was one luxury Rolls-Royce could no longer afford. The other closure was the company-owned service and repair department known as Western Avenue, where costly remedial work was carried out to mask inadequate manufacturing standards at Crewe. Rolls-Royce and Bentley clients in London were still well served through the dealerships of Jack Barclay, which had long established showrooms a few minutes walk away in Berkeley Square, and H.R. Owen in South Kensington.

Rolls-Royce was in the process of spending about £100 million on the new products and £50 million on factory modernisation. The sums would be trifling to a large car maker, but to Rolls-Royce they represented a huge commitment. Without the unpredictable, and distorting, income from the Brunei specials, Rolls-Royce was aware that it walked a financial tightrope in the mid-1990s. Its cost base, revolving around Crewe and its workforce of about 2,200, meant the company had to sell 1,800 cars a year. Worldwide annual sales gradually recovered, from just over 1,400 in 1994 to over 1,900 by 1997.

Meanwhile, the company's engineers were busy with the development of the BMW-powered replacements for the Rolls-Royce and Bentley. The project began life as the P600, which was given formal approval by Vickers in the middle of 1995. But in order to underline the differences between the brands internally, they soon became the P2000 (Rolls-Royce) and P3000 (Bentley). The difficulty was that the company had a bronze budget to achieve a gold standard in terms of brand differentiation.

The P2000, in addition to its V12 engine, featured suspension settings giving it a limousine feel. Its seats were softer and tyres were selected for a softer ride. The discrete exhaust pipes produced a purring noise. There was a column-mounted gear shift lever, but no rev counter. The radiator grille and flying lady statuette were pared down to be less intrusive.

By contrast, the P3000 had a V8 with twin turbochargers, a unit heavily reworked by Cosworth to produce an acceleration time from rest to 60 mph in less than six seconds. There was, of course, a prominent rev counter, complemented by other parchment-coloured instruments and more adventurous wood and other treatments for the interior. Everything was firmer, including the suspension, tyres and more wrap-around seats. The car had a centre console and a centrally mounted lever with sporty change-up points for the automatic. The large bore exhausts were highly visible and tuned to produce a distinctive V8 rumble. The egg box-style grille in brushed welded stainless steel was more aggressive.

The two models, which would make their debuts in early 1998, embodied features the company felt best constituted their DNAs. Rolls-Royces stood for endurance, grace, wisdom, endeavour and celebration. Bentley's characteristics were certainty, passion, daring, stamina and breeding. As a company, Rolls-Royce had clearly left behind the days when it could afford to ignore Bentley. The product-planning decisions made during the development stage reflected the reality of what was happening in the market place. The wealthy young whiz-kids with windfalls from software and telecom flotations were suddenly in a position to buy their BMWs and Mercedes, their Audis and Aston Martins, their Porsches and Ferraris. In many cases, Rolls-Royce owners were, literally, a dying breed.

Further evidence that the Bentley side was in the ascendant at Crewe came from the concept known as MSB, or Medium-Sized Bentley. Woodwark's vision was to offer a series of Bentleys – four-door saloon, two-door coupé and convertible – selling at prices ranging from roughly £75,000 to £100,000. The belief was that Bentley could and should provide a real choice in that market category, where buying a top-line BMW or Mercedes was becoming a cliché for new money and business success. The fact that Volkswagen came to a broadly similar conclusion when it acquired Bentley is an endorsement of the 1995 concept.

The MSB also had its origins in the 1994 Java mock-up that so excited Prince Jefri. However, once Vickers elected to go with the BMW solution to the P2000 and P3000 engine questions at the end of 1994, Bentley began casting around for a technology partner to transform its Java ideas into a more tangible working project. Bentley's MSB, later given the project name P1000, was based on the running gear of a BMW 5-series.

Bentley and BMW each assigned a dozen people to the project, housed a short distance from the German company's FIZ technology centre in Munich. The project team was completely self-contained with its own specialists in the fields of design, engineering, purchasing, finance and manufacturing. It was led by Tony Gott who worked on the project throughout 1995 in Munich. A prototype, which is apparently still at Crewe, was completed and a full business plan drawn up. But with the P2000 and P3000 under development, Rolls-Royce could never give any priority to P1000. The project was never formally presented to the Vickers board for approval, but it was still simmering when Rolls-Royce Motor Cars was overtaken by the dramatic sale decision in late October 1997.

The MSB is believed to have been technically and financially sound, but Vickers was always going to have a problem funding a smaller car as well as the P2000 and P3000. Another concern on the Bentley side was whether the prototype contained too much BMW and not enough Bentley, which raised issues about brand integrity and corporate ownership. For BMW, though, with its strategic vision of ultimate ownership of Rolls-Royce and Bentley, the exercise proved to be another excellent opportunity to edge closer towards its prize.

Working on assignment in Germany was not new to Gott. When Rolls-Royce started to look for an engine supplier towards the end of 1994, it was already familiar with the strengths of BMW. Rolls-Royce knew its engines were good but needed a technology yardstick as a lever to improve its bargaining position. What started as purely engineering discussions with Mercedes-Benz, BMW's great rival, ended with Gott and a small team from Crewe working on a practical project in Stuttgart in November and December.

In addition to the offer of Mercedes' V12 and the then-new V8 engines, the two sides came up with a proposal to use the chassis from the Mercedes S-class for Crewe's next large cars. The concept was based around the huge S-class launched in 1991, not the slimmed down replacement that appeared in 1998. While the older S-class was not a commercial success – it went on sale as the global sales recession struck – its greatly admired chassis and running gear were designed and engineered without compromise. It was also of the size and strength that would make an appropriate donor chassis for large Rolls-Royces and Bentleys. The Gott project team returned with enough evidence to convince the Rolls-Royce board that it should plump for Mercedes, even if it was ultimately defeated by Vickers and the political machinations of Rolls-Royce plc.

The Mercedes and P1000 exercises demonstrated that Gott had emerged as a distinguished engineer and manager. He became the project director for P2000 and P3000 in April 1996, engineering director the following April, and joined the board at the end of 1997. His priority was to make sure the Silver Seraph and Arnage appeared on time and on budget.

MEANWHILE, IN
THE OUTSIDE WORLD

The history of Rolls-Royce and Bentley in the 20th century can be seen as a microcosm of European society. Expensive craft-built cars made were initially the exclusive preserve of kings and counts, the all-powerful royals, maharajahs, aristocrats and the landed gentry who held so much influence over society. Later, the lower costs stemming from mass production allowed the middle classes to enjoy the pleasure and convenience of private cars. The working classes stayed at home, walked or went by bus. Car ownership today is within the grasp of most people in the world's developed countries, and a growing number in developing nations.

Democracy, meritocracy, travel, technology, globalisation and new means of wealth creation relieved the old money aristocracy of so much of its influence. A woman had become prime minister in Britain before the end of a century that began with women fighting for the right even to vote. The United States appointed a black secretary of state at the start of the 21st century, an appointment hitherto unimaginable in a country which so recently had practised segregation. As the 20th century evolved, new money and new ideas increasingly re-shaped society. So it was in the business of vehicle manufacture.

The spread of car ownership saw the steady decline, or demise, of the great car names favoured by the wealthy early motorists. Real power in the vehicle industry at the end of the century lay with the huge groups that answered the motoring needs of the common man. By the end of the 20th century, Rolls-Royce Motor Cars, despite its flowering Bentley marque, was an anachronism as an independent entity. Its names and historical achievements were admired, but, like the faded aristocracy, they were largely irrelevant in a modern world.

It was no surprise to find that the companies battling for ownership of the two distinguished British nameplates at the end of the century were not even in existence when Rolls met Royce in 1904. BMW, which began as an aircraft engine producer, did not venture into cars until it bought the manufacturer of the Dixi. Volkswagen was the ambitious 1930s product of a megalomaniac politician. Even Mercedes-Benz, generally acknowledged as the originators of the motor car, did not exist as such. The single company was formed in 1926 by the union of the rival Daimler (the maker of Mercedes cars) and Benz companies, which, unknown to each other, simultaneously began their first motoring experiments at opposite ends of the Neckar Valley in Germany in the 1880s.

But by the end of the century, the three German vehicle firms were international powerhouses in the field of road transport. Getting there required periodically leaping substantial hurdles but they succeeded by doing most things right most of the time. Overcoming the rubble and material privations of a country broken by war, they epitomised the German economic miracle.

BMW was founded in 1917 as an aircraft engine manufacturer and turned to motorcycles six years later. Its involvement with cars began in 1928 when it took over the troubled Dixi factory in the Thuringian town of Eisenach – a location that, when communism enveloped eastern Germany, became the home of the unloved Wartburg. From BMW's humble car beginnings as the producer of the 750 cc Dixi, a licence-built Austin Seven, its reputation quickly developed as a manufacturer of saloons and race-winning sports cars.

In the 1930s, it was impossible to stand back from Germany's political upheaval. BMW, drawing on slave labour from the nearby Dachau concentration camp, became a primary contractor to the

Nazi war machine, making engines for the Focke-Wulf 190 fighter, Messerschmitt 262 jet fighter-bomber and many other aircraft. The price it paid was a concentration on its factories by the Allied bombing campaign.

The post-war period was exceptionally difficult for BMW. It was a fine engineering company but no longer had a role. Instead of aircraft engines, it made items needed to rebuild the country: agricultural machinery, saucepans and bicycles. Motorcycle output resumed quite quickly, but the company was clearly in a dilemma about cars. It resumed its efforts to sell magnificent and expensive models like the 501 saloon and 507 roadster, but also produced bubble cars. Even with more mid-range models like the 1600 and 700, BMW was essentially bankrupt by the end of the 1950s. Negotiations for its purchase were held with, among others, Ford and American Motors and Britain's Rootes group. By December 1959, BMW was within 24 hours of being taken over by Daimler-Benz.

It avoided that fate due to the intervention of Harald Quandt, the industrialist whose family retains the largest shareholding in BMW. Quandt recruited Eberhard v. Kuenheim to work for the Quandt group in 1965, and in January 1970 made him chairman of BMW. The appointment was a surprise as much as it was inspired. At 41, v. Kuenheim was the youngest head of an industrial company in Germany.

More than any other person, v. Kuenheim created the modern BMW group. He took over an obscure, provincial car and motorcycle maker frequently confused by car buyers with BMC, which was then a group of considerable scale. Today, BMWs are worthy rivals to the models from the company that nearly bought it, Mercedes-Benz. BMW's style and image, its products and systems, its business performance and its global presence, were meticulously perfected during v. Kuenheim's 23 years at the top. When he retired, he was still able to keep a close watch on his successor from a position as head of BMW's supervisory board. That successor was Bernd Pischetsrieder, who negotiated the purchase of Rolls-Royce.

His failure to secure Bentley as well was due to the determination of Ferdinand Piëch, the chairman of Volkswagen. The maker of Germany's People's Car had come a long way since Piëch's father, Anton, was the company's first managing director at the end of the 1930s. Volkswagen's giant, purpose-built factory in what was then known as the Town of the Strength Through Joy Car (subsequently and more conveniently named Wolfsburg by the victorious Allies) in Lower Saxony never did make many of the cars that Chancellor Adolf Hitler promised his people before the world descended into chaos. Instead, it made small go-anywhere vehicles and amphibians for the military before two-thirds of the factory was destroyed by repeated daylight bombing raids.

No one knew what to do with Volkswagen after the war. British car makers and Henry Ford II rejected it with derision, convinced that air-cooled, rear-engined cars would never sell. So much for conventional wisdom. Major Ivan Hirst of the British Army held the venture together by using the factory to repair and service vehicles for the occupying forces and build Volkswagens for the German post office. But the Beetle legend was really born after Professor Heinz Nordhoff, who was appointed by Hirst, took over as the plant's general manager in 1948. Demand for Volkswagen cars and minibuses around the world soared. One million were made by 1955, 5 million by 1961 and 10 million by 1965.

By the time Volkswagen bid for Rolls-Royce and Bentley, it was the largest vehicle maker in Europe and the world's fourth largest group behind only General Motors, Ford and Toyota. It had established a major manufacturing presence across Europe, as well as in Brazil, Mexico, China and South Africa. It had bought Audi as long ago as 1970, and more recently added Seat of Spain and Skoda of the Czech Republic.

When Piëch took over as chairman from Carl Hahn in 1993, he instituted a series of measures that transformed the scale and structure of the Volkswagen group. Piëch's vision was for the Volkswagen group's products to match the technology, prestige and quality standards of other German car makers, essentially Mercedes-Benz and BMW. If they launched smaller cars to rival his Volkswagen Golf (the

Mercedes A-class and BMW Compact), then Volkswagen would challenge them with more luxurious models such as the Phaeton saloon and the Touareg sport-utility. Along the way, Piëch had the group buy Lamborghini and Bugatti in Italy. What was missing from the portfolio was a British prestige car brand.

The unknown was what Mercedes-Benz would do when – "if" no longer seemed likely – Rolls-Royce and Bentley came on the market. No one under-estimated Mercedes. Daimler-Benz, its parent group, was formed in 1926, a grim period of crisis and depression in Germany. However, the rearmament launched when the Nazis took office created tremendous business opportunities for an industrial group like Daimler-Benz. As with other firms, it used forced labour to manufacture aircraft engines, tanks and transport equipment, while suffering heavily from Allied bombing.

After the war Daimler-Benz slowly but surely regained its strength as a maker of cars, vans, trucks and buses. The reputation of its vehicles for quality, reliability and longevity gathered pace as it pushed into export markets. Mercedes' silver Grand Prix cars and long distance sports cars were for a period unbeatable on the world's race tracks, until the company abruptly withdrew from racing following the 1955 Le Mans disaster in which more than 80 people were killed when one of its cars flew into a spectator area.

By the time Mercedes celebrated its centenary in 1986, it was setting the car industry's benchmark in terms of engineering and prestige. The 1991 S-class saloon achieved quality and technology standards that Crewe could only dream about. But the S-class also exposed much of what was rotten within Mercedes. It was 18 months late to market and 50 per cent over budget. Decades of success had generated complacency. The economic recession in the early 1990s did not just affect Rolls-Royce. It hit Mercedes so hard that a new strategy was needed if the company was to survive.

Helmut Werner, recently appointed president of Mercedes, shocked the car world in January 1993 by saying his company's products were over-priced and over-engineered. It signalled the end of cost-plus engineering at Mercedes. In future, Werner declared,

Mercedes cars would be developed to a budget and be more afford-able. It would enter new market categories with models that over the following years turned out to be the A-class, M-class and V-class. What Werner revealed was the motor industry's equivalent of Saul's conversion on the road to Damascus.

However, barely noticed at the time, Werner also said Mercedes would develop an "extra large saloon". With the then-new S-class under attack by critics because of its weight and size, and demand for large cars in steep decline, it was impossible to conceive what the man had in mind. Neither was Werner forthcoming. Anything larger than Mercedes sold at that time could only mean a car in the Rolls-Royce category.

Mercedes, well aware of the technology-sharing agreement that BMW agreed the previous year with Rolls-Royce, had to consider what its strategy would be if BMW acquired the venerable British car maker. The two were, and remain, such rivals that neither could afford to ignore the other's initiatives. If BMW acquired Rolls-Royce and Bentley, Mercedes would have to respond. The first indication of what form that response would take came at the Tokyo motor show in October 1997, when the company unveiled a giant concept limou-sine known as the Mercedes-Benz Maybach.

The name resurrected a distinguished German luxury car mar-que, dormant since 1941. Carl Wilhelm Maybach was born in Cologne in 1879, 16 years after Henry Royce and two years after Charles Rolls. He was an engineer at Daimler before he and Graf Ferdinand von Zeppelin founded their own firm in 1909. Not per-mitted to build engines for airships or aircraft after the Great War, Maybach turned to cars. Starting in 1921, Maybach produced a total of 1,800 magnificent cars, including the 7-litre V12-powered Zeppelin of 1930. Maybach customers included the tenor Enrico Caruso, boxer Max Schmeling, Emperor Haile Selassie of Ethiopia and the Maharajah of Jaipur.

The remains of the company came into the Daimler-Benz fold in 1960, when it bought a majority holding in the engine plant in Friedrichshafen. Six years later, Daimler combined its own large engine production with that of Maybach. That company later became Motoren- und Turbinin-Union Friedrichshafen – MTU for short – which was best known as a producer of gas turbine aircraft engines. Most people, except historians, had forgotten the great Maybach name by the time it appeared on the Mercedes concept car in 1997. Even then, Mercedes was not sure what recognition it would have, so the concept was adorned by a Mercedes star rather than the double-M badge that production versions of the Maybach wear today.

However, between Werner's January 1993 announcement of the forthcoming Mercedes product offensive and the debut of the Maybach concept in October 1997, there was the BMW-Mercedes competition to provide engines for a new generation of Rolls-Royces and Bentleys. When BMW secured the agreement at the end of 1994, Mercedes' "extra large saloon" ideas took on greater significance.

Then, a week after the Maybach was unveiled in Tokyo, rumours again began to circulate in Britain that Vickers had returned to the idea of selling Rolls-Royce. When Vickers finally confirmed on October 27 its intention was to sell its luxury car firm, BMW emerged as the clear favourite. However, the world at large was not entirely convinced when Daimler-Benz, Ford, Fiat and Volkswagen each professed no interest in acquiring Rolls-Royce.

With the new generation of cars only a few months from launch, the most bizarre aspect seemed to be timing. Selling the company that made Rolls-Royce and Bentley was hardly a ringing endorsement, especially when it was on the verge of launching two critical new models. The sale would send mixed messages about the viability of Rolls-Royce and the prospects for its new models. But timing might also be critical for Vickers if it wished to maximise the value of Rolls-Royce. It seems to have decided that a period of rising demand for the cars after their launches would be best. The new Rolls-Royce was due in January 1988 and the Bentley four months later.

In addition, Vickers was in a poor bargaining position because of the constraints of the technology supply agreement with BMW. Under these circumstances, would any other vehicle maker be interested in Rolls-Royce, especially now Mercedes-Benz had declared its premium car intentions with the Maybach concept? Of course, whatever their public declarations, all major vehicle groups would have to consider whether to bid for Rolls-Royce, though Vickers had no indications about how serious they would be. The BMW grip on Rolls-Royce meant Vickers was in danger of having only one potential suitor. It needed a lot more outside interest in order to leverage the value of the company it was planning to sell.

While all this was going on, the City of London was simultaneously buzzing with news about Vickers selling its medical equipment arm and acquiring part of the defence business of GKN as part of a broad structural realignment. Then came a wholly unexpected development. On November 5, Vickers stunned the City by announcing that it was *expecting* a hostile take-over bid from Mayflower Corporation, the contract engineering firm with a capitalisation only half that of its would-be prey.

It was a symbolic as well as financial shock. Vickers was a bastion of British industry dating back to the early 19th century. Mayflower had been created less than a decade earlier through a reverse take-over of the maker of Triang toys.

Mayflower, founded by business entrepreneur John Simpson and City financier Rupert Hambro, did all its business in the motor industry, so it seemed unlikely its interest was in the tank-building subsidiary of Vickers. The Cosworth engine business might be an appropriate strategic fit, because Mayflower's expertise was in vehicle body engineering and assembly following a series of take-overs, including Motor Panels, International Automotive Design and Walter Alexander. As such, it had substantial contracts to supply body pressings for the forthcoming new Rolls-Royce and Bentley models, as well as supplying completed MGF body shells and other pressings to the BMW group through its Rover subsidiary.

Mayflower's share price quickly fell because of the borrowing implications in a £1 billion take-over of Vickers. The rationale behind its thinking was not immediately apparent, but still Mayflower kept its counsel. It clearly had something in mind, yet a bid was never formally launched. In the belief that Rolls-Royce was the real Mayflower target, not the parent Vickers group, conspiracy theorists were inclined to believe that Mayflower's action would have the effect of pushing up the value of Rolls-Royce. With only one known Rolls-Royce bid in the offing, that would be warmly welcomed by Vickers.

As it turned out, the BMW connection was to prove the undoing for Mayflower's ambition. On the evening of November 11, Mayflower announced that it had "no intention of bidding" for Vickers. However, the same statement said Mayflower reserved the right to bid for Vickers "if the position of BMW changes in respect of Rolls-Royce Motor Cars".

Mayflower was forced to revise its view of the automotive environment after BMW restated its position that, in the event of Rolls-Royce being taken over by another automotive company, a clause allowing it to withdraw the engine supply agreement after a year would be invoked. There was more. Mayflower was also reminded of its servant-master relationship as a supplier to the BMW group. If Mayflower stood in the way of BMW's grand designs on Rolls-Royce, Mayflower might need to find itself a new employer. It did the trick.

So, Mayflower was out of the running. Mercedes-Benz, with its new Maybach project bubbling up, insisted it was not interested, even though it secretly pursued its investigation of a possible Rolls-Royce buy-out. Various wealthy amateurs wrapped themselves in their Union Jacks, promising to keep the famous brands British thanks to generous funding from unspecified donors. For a few days, though, it looked as though Vickers would have only one serious active bidder at the Rolls-Royce auction – BMW.

The scenario changed dramatically on November 14, when Volkswagen finally confirmed a story published in *Stern* magazine a couple of days earlier. Yes, it was interested in buying Rolls-Royce. While the prospect of the People's Car company owning the Plutocrats' favourite car company was hard to grasp, it was the best possible news for Vickers. At last, it had a known and powerful rival to help drive up the value of Rolls-Royce Motor Cars.

For the German firms, the value of Rolls-Royce and Bentley was not their asset worth or technological leadership, but their rarity, their polish and their historic breeding. Modern car groups manufacturing models by the million had nothing to learn from them technically. But what Rolls-Royce and Bentley had was something the big groups never acquired, for all their achievements: class. It gave them a value far above their intrinsic worth.

CHAPTER 17

VICKERS CHANGES DIRECTION

Graham Morris and his wife, Shirley, treated themselves to a Caribbean cruise in October 1997 to celebrate their silver wedding anniversary. For Morris, the chief executive of Rolls-Royce, the holiday also provided a much-needed spell of relaxation after the rigours of a motor industry career living in South Africa, the United States and Germany. Morris had made 230 flights the previous year in his role as sales and marketing chief of Volkswagen's Audi subsidiary. Rolls-Royce in Crewe was much more convenient. Instead of the gruelling weekly commute to southern Germany, he enjoyed a daily drive of 20 minutes through the Cheshire countryside from his family home. Morris now knew he needed to gather his strength for what would be a demanding work schedule when he returned to Crewe and the imminent launches of the first new Rolls-Royce and Bentley models for 18 years.

Then an unexpected call on the ship's telephone instantly ended the idyll in the sun. The call was to change his life. It came from Keith Sanders, the sales and marketing director of Rolls-Royce. He wanted to know what Morris knew about the Vickers announcement in London that it had decided to sell Rolls-Royce Motor Cars. The short answer was, nothing. Morris's first reaction was one of anger, soon followed by shock, concern and confusion. When he had joined Rolls-Royce six months earlier, it was with assurances that Vickers had no intentions of selling the luxury car firm. Of course, Morris was fairly sure Rolls-Royce would be sold at some time in the future, but why now? Why not at least wait until sales revenue from the new cars began to repay the investment that would take them on to market in a few months?

Immediate thoughts about cutting short his holiday and flying back to Britain were abandoned. There was nothing Morris could do by returning early because Vickers' decision was made and the world already knew it. The embarrassing factor was that the company's chief executive was one of the last to find out about it. Morris decided to try to make the best of his ruined holiday, which became punctuated by daily ship-to-shore phone conversations with colleagues at Vickers and Rolls-Royce.

The decision to sell Rolls-Royce was probably good for the long-term future of the company. Competitive pressure was such that Vickers could never get away with another product life cycle spanning more than three decades. And the group was clearly not inclined to make the regular heavy investments needed to renew the Rolls-Royce and Bentley range. At least any new owner was likely to be a major automotive group that understood the car sector. The cavalier way Vickers handled the decision was seriously flawed, however.

By continuing his holiday, Morris had an opportunity to calm down and to collect his thoughts. By the time he returned to work, he knew what he had to do. After discussing the issue with Rolls-Royce directors and managers, Morris had to explain to the firm's 2,000-plus employees at Crewe what had happened, why, and what the future was likely to be.

He did so using one of the newsletters he wrote on a weekly basis as a means of improving communication between management and workforce. Newsletters of this type served Morris well throughout his career, starting from the time he was the young plant director at Speke, the BL assembly factory just outside Liverpool that was a hotbed of industrial conflict in the 1960s. To the puzzled and worried employees at Crewe, he wrote that the sale was a good development, even if the method of communicating it was not. The important task was to ensure good launches for the forthcoming new models. If that happened, whichever group bought Rolls-Royce was likely to look favourably on the company's frustrated scheme to add a second model to the range, the so-called Medium-Sized Bentley, or MSB.

During his first week back at work, Morris travelled to London for a meeting with Sir Colin Chandler, the chairman of Vickers. Chandler apologised to the Rolls-Royce chief executive for the way he learned about the sale of his company, but said the matter was out of Vickers' control because of the possible Mayflower bid. Morris was reminded that his loyalty was with Vickers until the moment Rolls-Royce was sold to its new owner.

Whatever happened, Rolls-Royce was going to the highest bidder. One former executive accurately summed up the sale as "the public prostitution of Rolls-Royce and Bentley". The sale put the Rolls-Royce people in invidious positions. They had to portray the company in the best possible light to maximise its value. They also had to be careful not to portray too rosy a picture because the new owner would quickly discover the truth once it took over.

Privately, Morris and a few close colleagues began to ponder the possibility of a management buy-out for Rolls-Royce. The idea was bounced off Vickers via Chris Woodwark, by then chief operating officer of Vickers and Morris's predecessor at Rolls-Royce. The two had previously worked together at Rover, and were all too familiar with the cash-consuming requirements of a marginal car company. Intuitively, they knew that in a few years' time an MBO group would face the same problems as Vickers had over the years. Purchasing the company was merely the down-payment. How could it fund a new generation of cars, let alone expand the product line-up with an MSB? The financial and technological requirements were so great that any such thoughts were soon put to one side. By contrast, the Phoenix consortium that bought the rump of the Rover group from BMW three years later came to a different conclusion.

As 1997 drew to a close, the grand sell-off strategy was orchestrated in London by Vickers and its financial advisers, Lazard Brothers. Simultaneously, the pressing need in Crewe was to make sure the new cars were ready for their introductions. It was important from a practical point of view because demand for the existing cars was tailing off in anticipation of their replacements. It was equally important for the self-respect of the company. It needed to get the new products and their market launches right, and it needed the new owner to know it as well.

One thing Rolls-Royce did know was that each newcomer would require far fewer hours to produce thanks to its more modern design and the different manufacturing approach. That would not signal cheaper cars, which in the cases of Rolls-Royce and Bentley might be self-defeating in terms of prestige and customer perception. It would mean better margins for the manufacturer. However, the labour content involved in the construction of a complex, highly appointed car like a Rolls-Royce will never resemble that of a mass-produced family car, which a modern, capital-intensive factory can comfortably turn out with 10 to 15 hours of labour. Nevertheless, the labour savings for Crewe's new cars were significant. While an existing Silver Spirit absorbed an average of 1,400 hours of labour to produce, it was calculated that one of the new Silver Seraphs would need only 450 hours. In reality, it took nearer to 600 hours, but it was still a huge cost-saving.

The company also knew the build quality of the newcomers would be better than that of the current models thanks to an audit system introduced earlier in the year. Superficially, all the polished wood, thick carpets and soft leather gave Crewe's cars a magnificent appearance. Reality did not match appearance. "The quality of the cars was as good as Ferrari's when I got there, but, compared with German luxury cars at the time, we had a significant opportunity to improve," Morris reflected in early 2003.

No one knew better than he did. Immediately before joining Rolls-Royce, Morris spent two years as board member responsible for sales and marketing at Audi in Ingolstadt, Germany. Audi was, and remains, obsessed by living in the shadow of its better established rivals, Mercedes and BMW. Everything Audi did over the previous two decades in terms of design, technology, performance and quality was aimed at dispensing once and for all with the historical reputation in its home market as a bit of a blue collar purchase. This meant being better than Mercedes and BMW, with which Audi constantly compared its products. When Morris left, he knew all about the quality standards at the German car companies.

The scientific system of static and dynamic quality evaluation introduced at Rolls-Royce was that devised by BMW, not because of the engine connection but because the German company made it available. It was another example of BMW making itself indispensable to Rolls-Royce. Tellingly, the system was the first of its type ever employed by Rolls-Royce.

With evidence from the formal quality audit, which embraced cars made by other companies as well, Rolls-Royce was able to address the areas that contributed to the standards of its finished cars. That meant suppliers of materials and components that went into Rolls-Royces and Bentleys, and the ability of the company's own workforce to build cars right first time. It required more flexible working practices than Rolls-Royce employees had been used to, but the aim was for the company to avoid all the costly and time-consuming rectification work after its cars were built. Using the measurements of the new system, Rolls-Royce says it was able to achieve a quality improvement of 30 per cent in only 10 months.

Activity at Crewe gathered pace in late 1997 as the launch deadlines drew near. It was not just behind the scenes in the workshops and on the factory floor. New products from Rolls-Royce and Bentley are extremely rare occurrences, so the company knew it would shortly be inundated by a steady stream of visitors. There would be civic and media groups, and distributors and dealers from around the world. There would also be a series of potential buyers, both of the new cars and of the company itself. Rolls-Royce decided it had to do something about the tired old reception area and car showroom in Pyms Road, Crewe. It is a fine piece of 1930s architecture, complete with curved staircases to the next floor, but totally neglected in the daily struggle for survival. It needed a fresh face to go with its new products and unknown new owner.

Each department was ordered to make savings from its budget to fund the remodelling. Conference rooms were added, and a small museum celebrating the sadly neglected histories of the two companies was commissioned. So sadly neglected, in fact, that much of the company's archive material was wantonly abandoned in refuse skips in the 1960s and 1970s. The car showrooms were refurbished to reflect the new format for Rolls-Royce and Bentley dealerships. The transformation, completed by January 1998, was achieved for the astonishing sum of only £400,000.

To entertain the expected parties of guests, Rolls-Royce also needed an appropriate auditorium and reception area. Ian McKay, the marketing director, came up with the idea of erecting a marquee within C-block, the new main assembly works, and an overhead tunnel to reach it from the refurbished reception area.

Honoured visitors were collected from their hotels in a fleet of old Rolls-Royces and taken to the Pyms Lane entrance for a black tie reception. From there, guests used the new tunnel to cross into the marquee area, where banked seating was arranged for a welcome and presentation about the new car, before the curtains parted for the first glimpse of the Silver Seraph. Then more curtains were drawn back to reveal to the surprised guests that they were in the heart of the Crewe factory. Following dinner at Crewe Hall, a Jacobean stately home that had been recently modernised, the visitors were returned to their hotels in a fleet of new Silver Seraphs. The real achievement was that Rolls-Royce managed to stage these impressive events for under £1 million, a fraction of the cost a large car maker would spend on anything similar.

The Rolls-Royce and Bentley were introduced separately in order to stress the differences between the two models. The Silver Seraph, powered by a 326-horsepower version of BMW's 5.4-litre V12, made its public debut at the Geneva motor show in March 1998 to the strains of Handel's *Hail the bright Seraphim* and an elegant performance by Deborah Bull, the Royal Ballet prima ballerina. The Arnage, which had the BMW 4.4-litre V8 developed by Cosworth with twin turbochargers to produce 354 horsepower, was unveiled the following month at the Le Mans race track in France. It was a symbolic return to the circuit where Bentley made its name in the 1920s and 1930s. No one in 1998 imagined that Bentley would be back at the race track as a competitor only three years later.

Morris's abiding memory of the period was an incident at the media ride and drive exercise for the Silver Seraph. The launch was based at Ackergill Tower, a superb private guest house on the rocky coast just north of Wick. Despite the January date, the weather was cold but clear. A beach party was organised after dinner, complete with driftwood fire, appropriate Scottish beverages and local melodies played on an accordion. The surreal part was watching Bull, the ballerina, take part in traditional Scottish dancing with Japanese journalists dressed in kilts and sporrans.

That was the fun part. Back in London, a nasty spat developed between Vickers and Rolls-Royce plc, the aircraft engine maker, over who owned the rights to the Rolls-Royce name when used on cars. The dispute, once more orchestrated by Sir Ralph Robins, was effectively an encore to the saga of the BMW versus Mercedes-Benz engine contract three years earlier. The reprise was to prove much more significant than anyone outside the companies involved could imagine at the time.

Working on Vickers' behalf, merchant bankers Lazards prepared the offer document that would decide the future of Rolls-Royce and Bentley. It was issued only to parties judged to be seriously interested. Media speculation about possible buyers was frequently ill-considered around that time. It seemed only necessary for some wealthy individual – Harrods boss Mohammed Fayed or Formula One motor racing tycoon Bernie Ecclestone, for example – to express a passing interest in the sale than the media had them bidding.

Through his advisers, Prince Jefri of Brunei expressed an interest in buying Rolls-Royce. But while the company was happy to sell Jefri and his entourage as many fabulously expensive vehicles as they wanted, it discouraged him from making a formal offer for Rolls-Royce itself. It knew only too well the technical, financial and manpower requirements involved in running a tiny manufacturing operation in competition with major international groups. No matter how wealthy, a capricious prince, who conducted his private and business affairs with an almost feudal attitude, would not be an appropriate owner of Rolls-Royce. Besides, there were signs across Asia in the autumn of 1997 that the big spending days were drawing to a close. Energy prices fell as, one by one, most of the region's key economies began to slide into recession.

Michael Shrimpton, a barrister, felt so passionately that Rolls-Royce and Bentley should remain British that he formed the Rolls-Royce Action Committee to raise funds for a private buy-out. His consortium of wealthy supporters was said to have access to plenty of money. But the group descended into in-fighting, resulting in Shrimpton being ousted by one of his would-be supporters, Kevin Morley. There was no love lost between the flamboyant Morley, another former Rover executive, and Morris, whom he intended to replace with himself if the consortium was successful. It was not, of course. Neither was the second private consortium Shrimpton then put together, though it succeeded in interrupting the Vickers extraordinary general meeting in June that finally voted in favour of Volkswagen.

BMW was clearly the favourite in the early stages because of its technical support for the car maker and its aircraft engine joint venture with the company that insisted it held the rights to the Rolls-Royce name. However, BMW chairman Bernd Pischetsrieder knew matters were not so clear-cut when he received a phone call in November 1997 from his old adversary at Volkswagen, Ferdinand Piëch. At that stage, neither company had declared its hand. The two watched each other like professional poker players, but it was evident both were interested. What Pischetsrieder had established in his own mind, though, was a top value for Rolls-Royce and Bentley beyond which he would not go. In other words, he knew if Piëch decided simply to outbid him, BMW would lose.

Daimler-Benz was another unknown quantity. Officially, it declared it was not interested in Rolls-Royce. But it still obtained a copy of the Lazard offer document and formed a study team headed by Dieter Zetsche, the board member responsible for sales and marketing, and supported by its financial advisers, Goldman Sachs. Indeed, on one particularly fraught occasion, a delegation from BMW arrived at Crewe one morning for a fact-finding tour, and a rival team from Daimler-Benz descended that afternoon on a similar mission. Rolls-Royce personnel successfully managed to keep the presence of each delegation secret from the other, though they had to keep reminding themselves which group they were talking to at any given time.

So, Daimler-Benz was much more interested than it cared to acknowledge in public. In the words of one insider, "Mercedes-Benz had a very serious run at it". It even went so far as to formulate a broad outline of its strategy for Rolls-Royce, which involved taking a minority shareholding for itself while Goldman Sachs would take the majority. Daimler's secret proposal to issue shares to employees was one that found a great deal of favour at the time at Rolls-Royce, which was under strict instructions from Vickers to remain neutral in all dealings with all prospective purchasers.

But it was not to be. The Daimler delegation abruptly pulled out of its Rolls-Royce investigations in early March with the enigmatic explanation that "there are other distractions". There were, but the world did not find out what they were until May, when the shock merger of Daimler-Benz and the Chrysler Corporation was revealed. A couple of venture capital firms went through the investigation process as well. So did JCB, the successful privately owned manufacturer of construction equipment run by Sir Anthony Bamford. While each delegation to Crewe was expected to act discreetly, the arrival of company founder Joe Bamford in a helicopter painted JCB yellow was a clear sign of his company's presence. JCB also withdrew.

The strain on Rolls-Royce personnel in the first quarter of 1998 was tremendous. All these top secret visits by would-be company buyers took place at the same time as the new Silver Seraph and Arnage were getting into production and while the company was promoting them with a series of parties for the media, worldwide distributors and potential customers.

By April, though, all the visitors had returned home and the new cars were coming out of Crewe. A clearer picture began to emerge. The ambitions of the private consortiums were mild distractions, but it was clear to Vickers the fight for Rolls-Royce and Bentley would be between the two big German vehicle groups, Volkswagen and BMW. Now it was time for a demonstration of corporate muscle flexing.

THE PLAYERS

T he race for Rolls-Royce Motor Cars pitted two of the world's
most respected automotive chief executives against each other.
The man in pole position was Dr Bernd Pischetsrieder, chairman of
the board of management at BMW in Munich. The outsider was Dr
Ferdinand Piëch, his opposite number at the larger Volkswagen
group based in Wolfsburg. Curiously, the two people who would ultimately decide the fate of the Rolls-Royce and Bentley brands knew
practically nothing about the international motor industry. They
were Sir Colin Chandler, the chairman of Vickers and a man steeped
in Britain's arms industry, and Sir Ralph Robins, the chairman of
Rolls-Royce plc, who spent his career in the aero engine business.
These, then, were the people who emerged as the principle players
after Vickers put Rolls-Royce into play in the autumn of 1997.

Pischetsrieder, or BP as he was known when he was at BMW,
studied mechanical engineering at Munich Technical University.
Early expectations of an academic life changed when he joined BMW
in 1973 as a production planning engineer. Several promotions later,
he was put in charge of production, development, purchasing and
logistics at BMW's plant in South Africa during 1982-85. He then
returned to Munich, and by 1991 had a seat on the group's board
with responsibilities for production.

Pischetsrieder's anointment as chairman two years later came as
a surprise. Outsiders expected the autocratic BMW chairman,

Eberhard v. Kuenheim, to nominate Dr Wolfgang Reitzle, another MTU alumnus, a year younger than Pischetsrieder and BMW's board member for R&D. But while Pischetsrieder criss-crossed the United States – under an assumed name for secrecy – in search of a site for the group's first car plant in the region, Reitzle flirted with an offer to become chairman of Porsche. Von Kuenheim regarded Reitzle's preparedness to join Porsche as a sign of disloyalty. And in large measure because of his role in successfully selecting Spartanburg, South Carolina, for the BMW factory, Pischetsrieder was rewarded with the top job.

The appointment was not on account of Pischetsrieder's appearance. Von Kuenheim, a formal Prussian of the old school, found it difficult to accept his replacement's precision-trimmed beard. Indeed, beards may be commonplace in the creative fields and in the new IT industries, but they are still extremely rare in an old fashioned metal-bashing industry like cars.

A few months after becoming chairman, Pischetsrieder made one of the most dramatic moves in BMW history: the surprise purchase in early 1994 of Britain's Rover group. The development, overseen by v. Kuenheim from his position as head of BMW's supervisory board, was uncharacteristic for the group. Apart from the 1966 take-over of Glas, the Dingolfing firm that made, among other things, the little Goggomobile, BMW had a policy of steady organic growth. There was no denying its success. But when Mercedes-Benz suddenly embarked on its major model expansion policy a year earlier, BMW had to respond. The Rover acquisition was a way of achieving similar economies of scale. The theory was that, by using the Rover, Land Rover, Mini and MG brands, BMW could create a portfolio of premium brands. The proposed purchase of Rolls-Royce and Bentley would complement them nicely, turning the group into an upmarket version of General Motors. BMW could cover all market segments like GM, but only at the premium end of each one.

History shows that, ultimately, the vision failed. The problems within the Rover group were so great they dragged down the business performance of BMW as a whole. The full extent of Rover's problems were not clear at the time Rolls-Royce was on the block, but they were shortly afterwards because of development delays concerning the new 75 saloon and the gathering strength of sterling. BMW's controlling Quandt family was not amused. It was used to handsome dividends from BMW and a steady increase in the value of its asset. When it ordered the break-up and sale of the Rover group, Pischetsrieder and Reitzle paid with their jobs in February 1999.

It was 18 months before Pischetsrieder resurfaced in the motor industry. Ironically, it was at the group with which he battled in early 1998 for ownership of Rolls-Royce and Bentley. In his memoirs, *Auto.biographie*, Volkswagen's Piëch wrote that he offered Pischetsrieder some sort of job at Volkswagen on the day the latter left BMW. It is hard to escape the notion that, out of those skirmishes for the two British brands, Piëch came to believe he had found the person who could succeed him as chairman of Volkswagen in four years' time. When Pischetsrieder became Volkswagen's broad member responsible for quality assurance – a newly created role – and chairman of its Seat subsidiary in Spain in July 2000, it was widely speculated that he would replace Piëch on his retirement. Indeed he did, on the day in April 2002 when Piëch turned 65.

Pischetsrieder is generally regarded as friendly and considerate, a top man who is prepared to carry his own bags. Unlike most German business people, he was happy at BMW to use a person's given name rather than the more usual family name, and to use the singular, more friendly du form of "you". He likes good cigars, and enjoys an occasional glass or red wine or beer. He is said to be able to read Latin and ancient Greek. Mountain-climbing and snowboarding are other pastimes, but, above all, Pischetsrieder likes cars, and the faster the better. An incident in one proved embarrassing. It led to an 18,000 German Mark donation to charity by Pischetsrieder after the crash of a $1 million BMW-powered McLaren F1 in which he was travelling.

But the very "niceness" of Pischetsrieder may have contributed to his downfall at BMW. To appease sentiment in Britain, where memories of the 20th century's two major conflicts can run deep, Pischetsrieder took a hands-off approach to Rover. He did not want

BMW to be perceived as the all-conquering German firm that took over the last vestiges of Britain's decimated volume car business. With hindsight, the decision was flawed. Rover needed much more robust handling. That very distance from Rover decision-making left the group with a product deficiency that came to haunt it after it became independent once more.

What are not in doubt, though, are Pischetsrieder's engineering qualifications. And, for an engineer, he has a remarkable understanding of the importance of branding. It was perhaps inevitable for anyone brought up in the BMW culture, and is certainly needed in a multi-brand group like Volkswagen. Neither are Pischetsrieder's deal-making abilities in doubt, as Piëch discovered in 1998.

Ferdinand Piëch was at the height of a long and distinguished career in the motor industry when the opportunity to buy Rolls-Royce and Bentley presented itself. It was impossible to resist. As the grandson of Ferdinand Porsche, the founder of the Porsche sports car and engineering contract firm, cars were part of Piëch's soul.

Piëch is also one of life's over-achievers. It was as if everything he undertook was to prove he was as good, or better, at his job than his famous grandfather, the man who designed the original Volkswagen Beetle. Piëch's case-hardened resolve was needed as soon as he took over from Carl Hahn as chairman of Volkswagen in January 1993. Volkswagen, he said at the time, was a "duck grown too fat to fly". The problem was that the group's biggest shareholder was the local government, the state of Lower Saxony. Ignoring the fact that Volkswagen employees are also voters, Piëch pushed through a massive programme of 36,000 redundancies and shortened the working week.

He decimated top management as well. Within a year of his arrival, directors in charge of finance, purchasing, design, R&D, commercial vehicles and worldwide sales were replaced. So were the deputy chairman and the heads of the Seat and Audi subsidiaries. Similar fates befell Volkswagen's top officials in the United States and Mexico. Terrified company managers even wrote anonymously to Volkswagen's supervisory board chairman, "Dr Liesen, this company is being 'led' by a man with psychopathic traits..."

The rottweiler reputation did not stem from Piëch's physique. The man is slightly built, short and balding. Rather, it came from his position as head of Europe's largest car maker and the utter conviction of his beliefs. His immense personal wealth from shareholdings in Porsche and in Porsche Holding, the Austrian company that distributes Volkswagen group products in most of central Europe, simply added to his confidence. Power, confidence and wealth are a formidable combination. Colleagues with mortgages and school fees to pay, work to live, but Piëch appeared to live to work. He certainly did not need to.

One mistake by an employee was tolerated, two were not, Piëch once acknowledged in an interview with the *Wall Street Journal*. Colleagues soon learned that it was not a career-enhancing move to question the chairman. While Piëch was unfailingly courteous to outsiders, what most people remember is the famous stare. Dave Woodruff interviewed Piëch a number of times when he worked for *Business Week*. "When he didn't like a question, he had a habit of staring at you with those grey-blue eyes and not answering. It was very unsettling," Woodruff recalled.

The record shows the Piëch formula was largely successful. The Volkswagen group sells in the region of 5 million cars world-wide, nearly three-quarters more than when Piëch became chairman. The cornerstone of his product strategy was a programme to reduce the number of the group's platforms from 16 to four to improve economies of scale. At the same time, he raised the quality of all products, particularly their interior finishes. As Volkswagen was Europe's leading car group, its rivals could not ignore the new standards. Piëch's quality initiatives therefore benefited car buyers everywhere.

Piëch's aim was simply for his group's stable of brands – Audi, Bugatti, Lamborghini, Seat, Skoda and Volkswagen – to make the best cars in their respective classes. When they did, customers and commercial success would follow. A former colleague recalled Piëch saying, "Great car companies are great because they make great cars and that's what I'm here to do. If I fail, I shall need great marketing people, and if they fail I shall need great accountants and lawyers."

Piëch's love of product, combined with an intolerance of dissent, produced problems, however. With no one brave enough to challenge the chairman's product knowledge, the Volkswagen group ended up making many similar cars during Piëch's era. For example, it brought out almost identical estate car versions of the Golf hatchback and Bora saloon, but missed the biggest market development in Europe, the growth of compact minivans after the launch of the Renault Scenic. Neither was Volkswagen able to match trend-setting models like the Renault Kangoo, Toyota RAV4 or Mazda MX5 in other sectors. At the time of writing, it was too early to judge whether Piëch's pet projects for complex, mega-money models like the Phaeton saloon and Touareg sport-utility would be successful. However, it seemed doubtful that sales would ever be sufficient to justify their development costs or the special factories in which they are made.

Before becoming chairman of Volkswagen, Piëch made his mark at Audi, where he was head of product engineering and then chairman. He pioneered the company's quattro four-wheel-drive system, its direct injection petrol engines, all-aluminium construction and fully galvanised steel bodywork.

Piëch was born in Vienna and studied engineering sciences at the Swiss Technical University in Zurich. It was almost inevitable he would join the family firm. He became Porsche's top engineer, and was responsible for the company's original flat-six engine. The 907 and 908 sports-racing cars of the 1960s were also Piëch products. So, more spectacularly, were the 917s that won the Le Mans 24-hours races in 1970-71. The racing regulations at the time required Porsche to build 25 identical 917s, a feat that drained the company's coffers. It is an indication of the money Piëch spent on racing at the time, because Porsche income included handsome royalty payments for grandfather's original design for the Beetle, then still very popular.

All good things must come to an end, however. When members of the Porsche and Piëch clan quarrelled in 1972 about who would run the company in the future and how, Porsche was turned into a joint stock company and all family members quit day-to-day management. It was at that stage that Piëch joined Audi.

A quarter of a century later, Piëch's (and Pischetsrieder's) attention was on stately limousines rather than fast cars. The man who stood between them and the cars was one of Britain's most successful salesmen. They knew he would drive a hard bargain.

During the late 1980s, Chandler, the Vickers chairman, was head of export sales at the Ministry of Defence. He led the team that secured the country's largest ever export deal: £20 billion worth of aircraft and military equipment to Saudi Arabia. The Al-Yamanah contract was won in the face of stiff competition with the French. Prime Minister Margaret Thatcher ensured he received a knighthood for his efforts.

Selling was in Chandler's blood. Earlier, there was a major contract for Hawker-Siddeley, his employers at the time, for Hawk trainers for the US Navy. When he joined Vickers in 1990, the British Army's order for Challenger II battle tanks was won against fierce competition from the Americans – and earlier technical problems with the Challengers.

Chandler told the *Financial Times* at the time of the Rolls-Royce sale that some psychological profiling tests by Vickers revealed him to be dominant, extrovert, impatient and impetuous. The assessment seemed about right. The square-jawed, solidly built Chandler was physically fit, keen on rugby and said to be a good *karaoke* performer. As head of a substantial public company in the engineering sector, he was a long way from his humble beginnings. Chandler was born in Rotherhithe, south-east London, to a tool-maker father and seamstress mother. He left school at 16 to take up an apprenticeship at De Havilland, the aircraft manufacturer. He worked for Hawker-Siddeley and the MoD before joining Vickers in 1990. As the group owned Rolls-Royce, it was Chandler's first exposure to the civilian world outside the arms trade. It did not look very appealing when he saw sales of Rolls-Royces collapse shortly afterwards, and Vickers' share price with it. Luxury cars were not an obvious complement to battle tanks. The car business would have to go when the time was right.

The person who held the key to Rolls-Royce was Sir Ralph Robins. It was the cause of intense irritation to everyone outside BMW involved in the fate of the car maker, especially Vickers and, as it turned out, Volkswagen. Robins joined Rolls-Royce as a graduate apprentice in 1955. He experienced the 1971 collapse and the subsequent separation of the firm's car division with which he had no direct connections. Robins' interpretation of that separation was that the rights to the use of the Rolls-Royce name and the interlocked Rs remained with the aircraft engine firm, whatever the product. That was not quite how it was seen by Sir David Plastow, the man who did the deal with the Official Receiver on behalf of the car company when cars was separated from aero engines. For him, the control was never going to be anything more than policing the use of the brand. It was never envisaged that the control of the brand would or could be used as a lever to manipulate future ownership, or to underpin an aeros-engine programme with BMW.

When Rolls-Royce Motor Cars was put up for sale by Vickers, Robins had been chief executive of the aero engine company for five years. By that time, his behind-the-scenes lobbying had engineered the agreement by which BMW, his company's partner in an aircraft engine joint venture, secured the engine supply agreement with Rolls-Royce Motor Cars, against the wishes of the car company itself. With the sale of the car company, he stood poised to repeat the trick for his old friends at BMW.

CHAPTER 19

A COSY COMPETITION

With hindsight, it seems like a tremendous fuss about very little. Two of the world's most powerful car makers were falling over themselves to pay good money for a company that considered itself very successful if it sold 3,300 cars a year. In 1997, the year Rolls-Royce Motor Cars was put on the market, sales were just over 1,900. When the deal was completed the following year, the total was down to 1,600 in spite of the attractions of all-new cars. There were several reasons why the figure was so low, starting with buyer reservations about whether it was appropriate for Rolls-Royce and Bentley to use bought-in engines for the first time in their histories. The sales slowdown also reflected the high-profile public prostitution of the two marques, which led to an erosion of buyer confidence. Then there was scepticism about whether any German company could understand the nature of Britain's traditional luxury car business. Many feared it would be a question of German Bauhaus meets English country house.

Still, BMW and Volkswagen were very interested in Rolls-Royce and Bentley. This posed another possible danger. The leading contenders were so big that the quaint old British brands were at risk of being smothered by the scale of the German firms. BMW employed 118,500 people worldwide in 1998, recorded car sales of 1.19 million and had group revenues of €32.3 billion. Volkswagen was bigger still. In 1998, it employed 298,000 people around the world, sold 4.75 million cars and had annual revenues of €68.6 billion. BMW sold twice as many cars *every day* as Rolls-Royce did *every year*. Volkswagen's daily sales were eight times larger than those of Rolls-Royce annually.

But a 3-series or a Golf is not a Silver Seraph or an Arnage. The premiums BMW and Volkswagen were prepared to pay were for the names, not the products. In early 1998, Vickers was about to discover how much the Rolls-Royce and Bentley names were worth on the open market, as opposed to a simple asset value in its financial statement. Considering it did not have the legal title to one of them, the first half of the year was to prove particularly rewarding for the group and for its shareholders. What it was definitely not was dignified.

The year began with a reminder from Rolls-Royce plc that it owned the name. Vickers contested that in an appeal to the European Commission, claiming Rolls-Royce plc was "abusing its licensing rights". It believed the stance was a bluff designed to win Rolls-Royce Motor Cars for the aircraft engine maker's business partners at BMW. That was the ultimate aim, but the motive was business, not bluff. In the absence of any clarification, the issue was mostly overlooked. It proved a mistake by everyone trying to understand the situation.

Michael Shrimpton's Rolls-Royce Action Committee declared its intention to raise £680 million to buy the car maker. Money of that sort could not have been ignored by Vickers, which expected bids in the region of £300 million to £400 million. Instead, Shrimpton was ejected from the consortium, whose eventual offer did not get it on to the short-list. Undaunted, Shrimpton began again with another private consortium, Crewe Motors, which he promised would raise enough money. To the surprise of no one except Crewe Motors, it failed to gain any assurances that its money was in place at the time it was needed. The professionals knew the nature of the international motor industry was no place for wealthy, well-meaning amateurs.

After the weeks of tiring, top secret to-ing and fro-ing, when the would-be owners of Rolls-Royce and Bentley gathered their intelligence and planned their strategies, the phoney war suddenly ended with a flourish of shots at the end of March. Here, at last, was some action. The first formal bid came from Volkswagen on March 25. It was followed a couple of days later by counter-offers from BMW and from Doughty Hanson, a secretive firm of venture capitalists, and from others unknown. Mercedes-Benz had already dropped out because of the need to concentrate on the still-secret Chrysler deal.

To the further surprise of everyone, within only four days, Vickers had apparently decided in favour of BMW. The unseemly speed of the decision-making tended to confirm what the sceptics believed from the start: that the open-bidding competition was a ruse to drive up the value of Rolls-Royce, when the decision had been made long ago to sell to BMW. It may have looked that way at the time, but that was not how it turned out. No one outside the chief executives of BMW, Volkswagen and Rolls-Royce plc had any concept at that stage about how the affair might end.

BMW's seeming victory was based on an offer of £340 million and promises to invest £1 billion in the business. The German car firm further said it would double the workforce to 5,000 and take annual output to 6,000 cars, which would be twice the level Crewe had ever achieved in its best years. The offer would further involve taking the stillborn small Bentley, the Java, to market and developing another Rolls-Royce project known as Bali. That was a proposal for a lightweight, aluminium-intensive derivative of the Silver Seraph and Arnage, which were constructed mainly of steel.

Vickers' provisional acceptance of the BMW offer, due to be put to shareholders at the annual meeting on April 29, effectively gave the German firm an exclusive, 30-day period to take an exhaustive inside look at the Rolls-Royce business. Volkswagen was thus shut out of the process, at least for the time being. However, what no one outside the top management of BMW and Volkswagen knew was that the two respective chief executives held regular discussions about how to resolve the issue in a way acceptable to them both.

Those talks dated back to November, shortly after Vickers erected the For Sale signs at Crewe. BMW was confident at the time it was in an excellent position to take over Rolls-Royce, though it was then apprehensive about what Mercedes-Benz was up to. The phone call from Volkswagen's Ferdinand Piëch therefore took Bernd Pischetsrieder by complete surprise. "I never came anywhere close to thinking that Volkswagen would be interested," Pischetsrieder acknowledged in early 2003. Once he found out, though, the chairman of BMW knew he faced a tough fight. He takes up the story:

"When Piëch phoned me once in November '97 and asked what my interest (in Rolls-Royce Motor Cars) was, I said to him that it was obvious that we would eventually consider making an offer. He said to me that they were interested as well, and he would mainly be interested in Bentley. I said to him that our marketing guys, which is important, were of the opinion that the two brands have to stick together and therefore I couldn't see a solution – to split the two brands voluntarily. The reason I said 'our marketing guys' was to give him the impression that this was not entirely my opinion, which at that point in time was not exactly the case. I knew, from a strategic point of view as much as Dr Piëch, that in terms of volume, Bentley was more interesting. Nevertheless, if BMW wanted to have in the group a car of the Bentley character it could easily have been a BMW-branded car – a 9-series or so – and the one car which would never have taken the name of BMW in terms of its character was a Rolls-Royce."

The conversation was the first of many discussions – on the phone and face to face – that Piëch and Pischetsrieder had during the manoeuvring for control of Rolls-Royce and Bentley. It is now clear that, far from being the bitter stand-off between the two German industrial giants it seemed at the time, the two chief executives were quietly working behind the scenes for a formula to divide the jewels to their mutual satisfaction. Very few of their senior colleagues were even aware of the discussions, as one who worked for Volkswagen discovered as the process dragged on. From the very start, for example, Volkswagen was made aware of the clauses in the Rolls-Royce and Bentley technology supply contract that BMW would withdraw its support after three years if a non-automotive group bought the British brands, and after one year if they went to a rival automotive group. Pischetsrieder again:

> "Piëch mainly concentrated then with his engineers on the engine question. They came to the judgment that, as far as the engines are concerned, they could look at this with the help of Cosworth. What was eventually, and finally, the stumbling block was actually the air conditioning unit, which could not have been replaced within one year. They initially thought they could force Behr, which delivers the component, to continue to supply directly, but this was obviously not possible due to the contract with BMW, as it was our design.
>
> We had many telephone conversations with Piëch before BMW put in a bid, and they were always focused around the question of whether we can possibly, without breaking the rules of the auction, make an acceptable solution for both of us. It didn't materialise because I insisted that BMW had the two brands. What Piëch publicly said, and no one ever believed him, was that he really only wanted Bentley."

Whatever the secret dealings in Germany, though, the position in Britain was that BMW had the month of April clear to complete its due diligence of Rolls-Royce Motor Cars, safe in the knowledge no other company could legally interfere. Going over the finances in more detail, BMW quickly discovered it would have to increase its offer by around £30 million because some of Rolls-Royce's liabilities were parked in the Vickers accounts. If the deal went through, BMW would therefore have to pay £30 million more than the £340 million it offered in the first place. It kept the information to itself. Cleverly, so did Andrew Johns, the finance director of Vickers, as Volkswagen ultimately learned to its cost. Determined not to descend into a bidding war over Rolls-Royce, BMW's position from the opening skirmishes was that its first offer would be its last. The additional £30 million might prove a useful bargaining ploy if Volkswagen's anticipated counter-offer was only marginally higher. Inside BMW, though, they knew from very early on that this single-bid policy would fail in the face of any determined opponent prepared to pay more.

It looked increasingly as if Volkswagen would be that determined rival. There were constant leaks that it was prepared to pay more, in spite of the recommendation by the Vickers board that BMW's offer should be accepted at the annual meeting, scheduled to take place at the London Arena in Docklands on April 29. Ominously, four days earlier, the Volkswagen supervisory board met to approve a higher offer for Rolls-Royce. Just how much more would not be revealed until after Vickers' AGM.

The annual meeting was an acrimonious affair. Despite the promise by Sir Colin Chandler, the Vickers chairman, that £197 million of BMW's money would be returned to shareholders, private investors present were not in a mammonist mood. Sentiment ran high, and they wanted Rolls-Royce and Bentley to remain British. Nicholas Bannister noted in the *Guardian* that the criticism appeared to bounce of Chandler "like small arms fire off one of the group's Challenger tanks". Chandler could afford to be impervious to the criticism because he knew he had the all-important backing of institutional investors. The motion was approved: Rolls-Royce Motor Cars would be sold to BMW.

Of course, it wasn't. Eight days later, the Vickers board was forced to change its mind by the sheer scale of the counter-bid from Volkswagen. Volkswagen accepted all the clauses and conditions of the BMW offer and said it was prepared to pay £90 million more than its rival. In other words, Volkswagen's proposal was for £430 million, or nearly 40 per cent more than its original offer and at the top end of any expectations by Vickers. When the board performed its U-turn with a recommendation that shareholders accept the Volkswagen plan, the lure was an 80 pence per share pay-out rather than the 55 pence under any sale to BMW. On top of that, there was a Volkswagen promise to invest £1.5 billion in Rolls-Royce and Bentley and to raise annual sales volumes to nearly 10,000 over the longer term.

The following day, May 8, it was announced that Chris Woodwark, Vickers' chief operating officer and a former head of Rolls-Royce and Cosworth, was to become chief executive of Staveley Industries. It was perhaps not a surprise. From the moment Vickers decided to sell Rolls-Royce – and Cosworth as it later emerged – Woodwark was effectively working himself out of a job.

The survival of the earlier BMW/Vickers agreement looked unlikely in the face of Volkswagen's very attractive counter-proposals. That was in spite of another reminder from Rolls-Royce plc that it, not Vickers, held the legal title to the use of the Rolls-Royce name. What still irritates at BMW is that Vickers did not keep its promise, made at the time, to alert the German group if there was an alternative bid. The phone call was never made. While BMW maintained it would stick to its one-bid policy, it knew it had some flexibility to increase its offer because of the Vickers loan guarantees found in the Rolls-Royce figures.

However, BMW was not taken by surprise when details of the Volkswagen offer began to appear in the media in early May. This was because Piëch told Pischetsrieder the amount Volkswagen was prepared to pay for Rolls-Royce Motor Cars before formally communicating it to Vickers. At that point, Pischetsrieder recognised that his strategy to buy both brands for BMW was at an end. The group was not prepared to join a bidding war, but it equally knew Volkswagen would never get its hands on Rolls-Royce.

By the time the world began to learn the details of Volkswagen's offer, Pischetsrieder had already flown to London to make an outline deal for the use of the Rolls-Royce name on cars with Sir Ralph Robins, the chairman of Rolls-Royce plc. The agreement was not formally signed until early June, by which time Vickers shareholders had overwhelmingly voted for the Volkswagen take-over of Rolls-Royce Motor Cars. What they did not know was that, in reality, they were approving the sale to Volkswagen of Bentley Motors.

The Pischetsrieder/Robins pact remained secret right up to the London press conference at the end of July, when the break-up of Rolls-Royce and Bentley was revealed to a stunned audience. One other person did know, however. That was Piëch. And he knew because, in the spirit of German collaboration that was a hallmark of the Vickers sell-off, Pischetsrieder told him.

CHAPTER 20

VOLKSWAGEN WINS HALF THE BATTLE

The Rolls-Royce car-licensing agreement was not the only topic discussed by Pischetsrieder and Robins at that time. Whatever the outside world believed, the BMW chairman was comfortable in the knowledge that he had secured the Rolls-Royce name for car use. But he still hankered after Bentley, and Robins, his opposite number at Rolls-Royce plc, seemed prepared to help his old business colleague. But how could they achieve this? Time and ideas were in short supply. The Vickers extraordinary general meeting to decide the final fate of Rolls-Royce Motor Cars was days away. Scheduled for June 5, it looked to be a gentle stroll to the winner's circle for Volkswagen because of its generous settlement proposal.

The bold concept Pischetsrieder and Robins came up with was to buy Vickers itself. They would share the costs and then divide the group, BMW taking over the automotive businesses and Rolls-Royce plc the defence and marine propulsion divisions. But while the broad concept was sound, the scheme needed much detailed work. Because the target was market-sensitive, it also required utmost secrecy. For BMW, there was an additional need for secrecy. The scheme would be scuppered if Volkswagen, seemingly headed for victory in the fight for Rolls-Royce Motor Cars, learned about the BMW project. Members of BMW's supervisory board were not even told about the investigation. Pischetsrieder and Robins called in their specialists, Dr

Hagen Lüderitz, the BMW legal counsel, and Rolls-Royce chief executive John Rose, to do the groundwork. They ensconced themselves in the London headquarters of BMW's investment bank, HSBC, which, as Samuel Montagu, acted as financial advisers to BMW in the 1994 Rover purchase.

The City of London is quiet outside the working week, and was particularly so over the weekend of May 23-24 with the following Monday a bank holiday in Britain. However, a glance out of the window provided a constant reminder of the need for vigilance. Across the River Thames stood the global headquarters of the *Financial Times*, a newspaper that would have had a keen interest in the secret deal being hatched in the HSBC building.

The two sides fairly quickly agreed how much they would offer: a 30 per cent premium over Vickers' Friday closing price, valuing the group at around £1 billion. As Lüderitz and Rose haggled over the details throughout Saturday and into Sunday morning, the framework for a formal bid ebbed and flowed. By around mid-day on Sunday, though, the two men felt sufficiently confident to summon their respective chairmen. Pischetsrieder flew by company jet from Munich to arrive at HSBC around 6 pm.

The four BMW and Rolls-Royce executives, together with their financial advisers, negotiated for another five hours or so. Both sides were aware of the historical sensitivity of a German firm owning a major British defence contractor, so how they planned to split Vickers was clear. BMW would end up with Rolls-Royce Motor Cars, Bentley Motors and Cosworth Engineering, and Rolls-Royce plc with the KaMeWah marine propulsion and Challenger main battle tank businesses. What they appear to have been unable to agree on were the risks and precise financial commitment each side would undertake. They were close, but not close enough. At around 11.30 pm, the proposed Vickers take-over was abandoned and the press conference, booked for the following morning, cancelled.

For BMW, it was the end of the Vickers episode. It was within a couple of weeks of losing the sale of Vickers' luxury car business to Volkswagen, even though BMW had a separate, and still secret, agreement to use the Rolls-Royce name. For Rolls-Royce plc, though, the aborted Vickers take-over proved to be an opening gambit. In September of the following year, Rolls-Royce plc bought what remained of Vickers for £933 million in cash, close to the amount it and BMW decided Vickers was worth when it included the luxury car and engine consultancy businesses. Three years later, in August 2002, Rolls-Royce then sold the tank business to Alvis while retaining the marine propulsion division. Vickers, a cornerstone of Britain's heavy industry dating back to the early 19th century, was no more. One way or another, though, its shareholders did exceptionally well out of the group's break-up.

Back in 1998, the war of words continued as the date of the critical June 5 extraordinary general meeting approached. As far as the outside world was concerned, Volkswagen now appeared assured of acquiring the Rolls-Royce and Bentley business, despite the proposal not having been endorsed by Rolls-Royce plc. As we now know, it never would be because of the secret deal stitched together by Pischetsrieder and Robins over the use of the Rolls-Royce name. It would be nearly two months before the impact of that hit the headlines.

Volkswagen then appeared to secure the Rolls-Royce and Bentley acquisition on the eve of the EGM by signing a letter of intent to purchase Vickers' Cosworth Engineering subsidiary. The offer of nearly £120 million, made through Volkswagen's Audi subsidiary, was conditional on Vickers shareholders accepting the Volkswagen proposals for Rolls-Royce and Bentley at the following day's EGM. The chances of shareholders rejecting a cash windfall from Volkswagen of nearly £600 million looked extremely remote.

BMW was asked whether it was also interested in Cosworth. It rejected the idea because of the company's huge motor racing commitment to Ford, and because it felt Cosworth's patented Zircon sand-casting process was too costly to be competitive.

The Vickers EGM was held amid tight security at the Royal Horticultural Society Halls in London. Like the AGM a few weeks before, the meeting was an emotionally charged affair in which small shareholders took the opportunity to berate the Vickers board for selling the country's automotive crown jewels to what they saw as the enemy. Vickers management was accused of selling "the birthright of British industry". Another shareholder said the British decision to hand back the Volkswagen works to Germany after the Second World War should now be repaid by Volkswagen allowing Rolls-Royce to remain British.

The sentiments were those of people whose calendars were pasted down in the Edwardian era. Yes, it was sad for Britons that Rolls-Royce and Bentley were in the process of being sold to foreign companies, but the change reflected reality. The facts were that the jewels being sold were chipped and tarnished, that Britain and Germany were fellow members of the European Union, and that Britain's motor industry was a post-national amalgam shaped by globalisation, sector consolidation and domestic failures.

And, of course, there was Michael Shrimpton, now leading another consortium called Crewe Motors. His claim to have secured promises of cash worth £490 million could not be ignored by Sir Colin Chandler, the Vickers chairman, however much of a diversion it would prove. In the knowledge that he could rely on institutional investors, if not private ones, to vote for the Volkswagen offer, Chandler called for an adjournment. This gave time to examine the validity of Shrimpton's claims he had the necessary finance lodged in the Bahamas and Switzerland, locations every bit as "foreign" as Germany. However, Vickers failed to find the proof it needed that the funds were in place.

When the meeting reconvened, Graham Morris, the Rolls-Royce Motor Cars chief executive, spoke on behalf of the beleaguered employees at Crewe. The best long-term solution for Rolls-Royce was to merge with a larger car group, he said. Morris pointed out that Volkswagen's £430 million had to be regarded simply as a down-payment. Much, much more would be needed to launch new models. If shareholders voted for the Shrimpton proposal, Morris told the meeting, he would resign and intimated that his fellow directors would follow suit. Under those circumstances – the lure of the

Volkswagen money and the threat of a management walk-out if the Crewe Motors proposal was adopted – there were more than 5 million votes for the Volkswagen motion and just 109,000 against.

Rolls-Royce Motor Cars and Cosworth Engineering went into limbo for a month while Volkswagen scrutinised their businesses. Technically, the companies were still part of Vickers until the moment Volkswagen, satisfied that all was in order, handed over the money. The German firm soon established the extra Rolls-Royce liabilities that BMW had earlier uncovered, so the amount it eventually paid was in excess of £470 million. Both purchases went through by early July. Shortly afterwards, one of the loose ends associated with the Cosworth purchase was resolved.

One of Cosworth's primary businesses was the design and manufacture of Formula One and CART motor racing engines for Ford. That would obviously be inappropriate when the company formally became part of Audi. The solution was for Ford to buy the racing division, which it did for an undisclosed sum, to become Cosworth Racing. The remaining road car engine consultancy business, contract engine assembly, and casting operations then came together as Cosworth Technology, an Audi-owned company.

As the Vickers-Volkswagen interregnum progressed, Morris began to alert his colleagues to the way life was about to change at Crewe. When Rolls-Royce was part of Vickers, it was more or less master of its own destiny. With the new owner, it would be part of a giant automotive group with complex, cross-functional disciplines. For example, all senior managers at Volkswagen's various car divisions regularly test drove other divisional products as well as those of competitors. Soon, engineers from Bentley would have to put Skodas through their paces, and know the strengths and weaknesses of each one.

The changes would be a shock to anyone cloistered in the legacy of Crewe's lofty past. Morris also knew something about the expectations of the driven man who headed the Volkswagen group from his period at Audi. Everything, he said, would be more demanding under Volkswagen. It would expect nothing less than excellence.

Ownership by a giant automotive group rather than a smallish general engineering group would mean a way of life never experienced at Crewe. True, money would soon be available for all the projects the company was never able to afford under Vickers. But as automotive professionals, Volkswagen would ask all the right questions. There would be nowhere to hide. Rolls-Royce personnel would not be able to flannel the new parent company, as it had the old one on occasion.

Budgets and product strategies began to be drawn up on the basis that the supply of BMW engines (and other components) would shortly disappear. It was an almost impossible exercise. The new Rolls-Royce and Bentley, on sale for only a few months, relied totally on components BMW was entitled to withdraw a year after ownership of Rolls-Royce Motor Cars passed to a rival car maker. That meant July 1999, but the Volkswagen group's own multi-cylinder engines would not be available by then. The answer was to resurrect the old 6.75-litre pushrod engine and, with an intensive and very costly development programme, make it comply with forthcoming emissions regulations.

The Rolls-Royce and Bentley product plan was also based on the assumption that Volkswagen owned both brands. As only Pischetsrieder, Robins and Piëch knew, it did not. The destiny of Bentley was clear, but ownership of the Rolls-Royce brand was publicly acknowledged by Volkswagen as an unresolved issue. In fact, it had privately been resolved by the pact between BMW and Rolls-Royce plc. The threat to suspend the supply of BMW components therefore made it an issue between Volkswagen and BMW rather than between Volkswagen and Rolls-Royce plc. And that was what Pischetsrieder and Piëch were secretly negotiating to resolve.

Each Monday for about five weeks, Piëch went to Munich to discuss some sort of compromise with Pischetsrieder. No one else was involved in the meetings, or was even aware of them. Piëch knew Pischetsrieder had secured the rights to the Rolls-Royce name, but Volkswagen's pending purchase of Rolls-Royce Motor Cars would provide it with certain assets wanted by BMW. Most of all, BMW really needed to be able to use the traditional Spirit of Ecstasy statue on its future Rolls-Royces. Unlike the famous double-R logo, which is used on cars and aircraft engines and belongs to Rolls-Royce plc, Charles Sykes's statue was used exclusively by the car division. It was therefore part of the Rolls-Royce Motor Cars package that was about to change hands.

BMW also wanted to own the car model names from Rolls-Royce history. In all cases except one, lineages were not in dispute. Silver Ghosts and Phantoms were exclusively Rolls-Royces, just as Red Labels and Continentals were Bentleys. The complication, still unresolved by the time Rolls-Royce left Crewe, concerned Corniche, a name used by Rolls-Royce and Bentley. All the names, though, belonged to Rolls-Royce Motor Cars, previously known as Rolls-Royce Motors and before that simply as the Car Division. Volkswagen would not want the Rolls-Royce memorabilia, but it knew they represented something of value to BMW. The negotiations, then, were not as one-sided as was suggested by the known threat by BMW to end component supplies for the Silver Seraph and Arnage.

Another possibility discussed was whether Volkswagen should continue to manufacture the Silver Seraph and BMW to market it. Pischetsrieder recalled, "The question always was, if the volumes which were in the bid were not met, who is to carry the losses? We were pretty sure that the volumes were overstated by 100 per cent, which in fact turned out to be right." What no one could determine was whether the lower sales were because of the car itself, or the controversy surrounding the sale of the company.

The series of top level meetings made steady progress until early July when *Sud Deutsche Zeitung* published an article outlining the *impasse* between Volkswagen and BMW over the future of the engine supply agreement. The article contained a number of quotes from Dr Klaus Kocks, the head of the Volkswagen group's communications department, commenting in strident terms that Volkswagen would do all it could to harm BMW if it withdrew. Unknown to Kocks, of course, his boss was surreptitiously involved in talks to resolve the situation amicably. Pischetsrieder found Kocks' tone so offensive he immediately despatched a fax to Rolls-Royce Motor Cars giving notice the engine supply agreement would be terminated in one year. The effect of the Kocks' comments was to strengthen the BMW bargaining stance: Volkswagen aggression rather than BMW intransigence was seen to bring the supply agreement to an end.

The threat of that withdrawal hung over Rolls-Royce from the moment it became clear Volkswagen had won the bidding war, but it was not exercised because, behind the scenes, Pischetsrieder and Piëch were still talking. When the termination notice arrived in the purchasing department at Crewe, the news spread instantly through the factory. Morris alerted Piëch, who tracked down Pischetsrieder. Was there any point in the following Monday's scheduled meeting taking place, Pischetsrieder asked. Yes, there was, replied Piëch.

The termination notice served to focus the minds of Pischetsrieder and Piëch. Both sides needed a face-saving formula to terminate the protracted and unseemly stand-off. Over the weekend before Monday's scheduled meeting with Piëch, Pischetsrieder came up with a framework he hoped might work. BMW would cede the rights to Rolls-Royce to Volkswagen on a temporary basis. That would leave Volkswagen with any financial liabilities if Silver Seraph sales failed to live up to forecasts, as well as provide BMW with enough time to create an entirely new Rolls-Royce from scratch. While the car industry is now familiar with the compromise, the interpretation was initially difficult for everyone to understand. Nothing like it had been tried before.

Pischetsrieder bounced the idea off Hagen Lüderitz, BMW's executive director, and then put the proposal to Piëch at Monday's scheduled meeting. Piëch liked the concept enough to agree to put it to the Volkswagen board meeting scheduled for the following day. When Piëch phoned Pischetsrieder after the meeting, it was to say they had a framework for the agreement. A meeting was then arranged for the following Monday at which Pischetsrieder and Lüderitz of BMW and Piëch and Volkswagen's top strategist and legal officer, Jens Neumann, finalised the details. They included the transition date – January 1, 2003 – and the transfer of the rights to the Spirit of Ecstasy and traditional Rolls-Royce model names to BMW.

When all the outstanding items were checked off by both sides, Volkswagen and BMW at last had a final agreement over the future of Rolls-Royce. The period of uncertainty and anxiety, which began when Vickers put Rolls-Royce Motor Cars up for sale the previous October, was about to end. The rest of the world, including the thousands of employees and countless other people who did business with the companies, did not find out until the media briefing suddenly called at the end of July.

Shortly before that happened, BMW received an unexpected counter-proposal from Volkswagen. Would BMW consider swapping Rolls-Royce for Bugatti? The car-making rights to the Bugatti name had been acquired in June by Volkswagen from Italian entrepreneur Romano Artioli, whose own attempt to resurrect the famous French marque ended in a 1995 bankruptcy. BMW's board talked about the matter over lunch one day, but rejected the idea. The company had already secured Rolls-Royce, and, by the end of the 20th century, Bugatti was virtually unknown. The wonderful Bugattis of the 1920s and 1930s were known only in car enthusiast circles, and Artioli's ambitious enterprise of the 1990s made no impact on the premium car market. And hanging over Bugatti was a question mark of the type that proved so troublesome to Volkswagen: the ultimate rights to the Bugatti name were not clear. They appeared to be dispersed between the French and Spanish arms of Hispano-Suiza.

In August, when the Volkswagen-BMW deal over Rolls-Royce was completed and its implications were being digested by a startled motor industry, Bernd Pischetsrieder suddenly realised he had overlooked something very important. He had forgotten to buy AX 201, the most famous Rolls-Royce of all time. The original Silver Ghost of 1906, arguably the most valuable car in the world and generally referred to by its registration number, remains the property of Bentley Motors. Now that Pischetsrieder is chairman of Volkswagen, the owners of Bentley, he has no intention of selling it to his former employers at BMW.

CHAPTER 21

THE TURNING POINT

Nowhere was the impact of that hastily arranged press confer-ence on July 28 felt more strongly than in Crewe. The town was first associated with Rolls-Royce when the aircraft engine factory began to be constructed in 1938. Crewe became the one-and-only home of the car-making side of the business in 1946. The plant in Pyms Road was known affectionately throughout the town as "Royce's". Now it was to become Bentley. There was nothing wrong with Bentley, but the scheduled exit of Rolls-Royce was akin to suf-fering a death in the family.

For the second time in his short career at Rolls-Royce Motor Cars, Graham Morris was wrong-footed by the machinations of a parent company. First, it was the shock of learning, despite earlier reassurances by Vickers, that the company of which he had been chief executive for only seven months was to be sold. He then spent nine months assuring employees, suppliers, dealers and customers that, whatever the outcome of the sale, Rolls-Royce and Bentley would not be separated.

The company had already been taken over by Volkswagen, but the sudden arrival in early July of the technology supply termination notice from BMW puzzled everyone. Morris was therefore under-standably apprehensive when he was phoned on Friday July 24 to be told he was required at a meeting at Volkswagen headquarters in Wolfsburg on Monday. The company would send a plane for him to a private airfield in North Wales. On arrival in Wolfsburg, Morris was presented with documents to sign. Reading them, he realised for the first time that Rolls-Royce would be leaving Crewe. As chief executive of Rolls-Royce Motor Cars, he was the only person who could legally put his name to the documents that would transfer the Rolls-Royce name to BMW. He had no choice but to sign.

Morris returned to his Cheshire home that evening with a heavy heart. Early the following morning, he took a train from Crewe to London to attend the press conference revealing the split to the world. At the same time, the Volkswagen executive jet carrying the two rival German teams arrived at Northolt from Manching. Their day had begun with the 7 am meeting at the deserted golf course in Bavaria to sign the agreement. With Pischetsrieder were Lüderitz and Richard Gaul, BMW's head of public relations. Piëch had Neumann with him. Wisely, in view of the animosity felt by Pischetsrieder towards Klaus Kocks after the outspoken comments published in *Sud Deutsche Zeitung*, the Volkswagen public relations department was represented by Kocks's deputy, Kurt Rippholz. When the twists of fate resulted in Pischetsrieder becoming chairman of Volkswagen just under four years later, Kocks left the group.

As the media representatives made their way to the hastily summoned meeting at the Institution of Civil Engineers in London that Tuesday morning, the principal players – Pischetsrieder, Piëch and Ralph Robins, the *eminence grise* from Rolls-Royce plc – chatted over coffee and biscuits in an ante-room. Tellingly for such an important business agreement, it was the first time Piëch and Robins had met, Volkswagen's attempts to negotiate the rights to the Rolls-Royce name having been led by Dr Robert Büchelhofer, the board member responsible for sales and marketing. The little group was joined by Morris, who was only too aware that orders for his cars had dropped by 30 per cent during the protracted and very public debate about their future. He made a last-ditch effort to persuade Piëch and Pischetsrieder to keep the development and production of the two brands together at Crewe. It was to no avail. Larger forces were at work.

Pischetsrieder and Robins looked immensely pleased with their agreement during the lively press conference. Piëch, by contrast, appeared strained, though the man's mien is invariably dour and inscrutable. The world's fuzzy understanding of what was going to happen to Rolls-Royce finally began to clear. The earlier Vickers sale of Rolls-Royce Motor Cars (incorporating Bentley Motors) for what eventually turned out to be nearly £480 million was confirmed. Well, almost. Volkswagen got the Bentley nameplate, the car factory at Crewe, its supplier contracts, its global distribution chain and its workforce of 2,500 people. It did not get the big prize because the Rolls-Royce name was not Vickers' to sell.

The separate agreement to use the Rolls-Royce name on cars was secured by BMW with a payment of £40 million to Rolls-Royce plc. And that was all BMW got. To sell a Rolls-Royce, BMW would need to design and develop a new model, recruit a work force, build an assembly plant, and create a supplier base and distribution network. For that, it would need time. BMW therefore elected not to activate its Rolls-Royce rights for the following 53 months. Until December 31, 2002, Volkswagen would be allowed to build and sell cars using the Rolls-Royce name. After that, the name would be taken up by BMW.

Piëch acknowledged that there was much more BMW technology in the latest Rolls-Royce and Bentley models than anyone at Volkswagen initially understood. Privately, he knew his company would give priority to replacing the Bentley's BMW 4.4-litre V8 engine with Crewe's traditional 6.75-litre V8 until Volkswagen's own engines were ready. It was a relatively straightforward, if expensive, exercise. However, Volkswagen would still need to use BMW's electronics and air conditioning system.

Piëch said he would have preferred to retain both brands, but that his real prize was Bentley. Most observers at the time saw the explanation as a face-saving excuse, but the evidence that emerged since then confirms that Bentley was, indeed, Piëch's primary target. He promised that Volkswagen would invest £1 billion in Bentley over the following decade and expand sales to 10,000 a year. This target was three times greater than anything the Crewe factory had achieved in the past with both brands, so it would be a daunting task. The cornerstone of Volkswagen's expansion strategy would be an all-new Bentley series that was initially known as MSB, or Medium-Sized Bentley. When it subsequently became clear that the new model was anything but "medium-sized" the term was quietly abandoned. While the model's stated volume ambitions were later scaled back, they indicated that the new range would be considerably cheaper than anything then sold by the company.

By contrast, Pischetsrieder was in an expansive, ebullient mood. He promised Rolls-Royces would continue to be made in England after BMW assumed responsibility for the brand. And he did mean England, not Britain, he emphasised. His comment raised the hopes of local authority development departments across the country, and led to media speculation that Rolls-Royces could be made in one of the facilities of the Rover group, then part of BMW. Even at the time, using Rover facilities was unlikely. When BMW walked away from Rover the following year, it became impossible.

Pischetsrieder indicated that annual Rolls-Royce sales volumes under BMW would be in the 1,500 to 2,000 range. The forecast was gradually eased back over the years, so by the time the new generation Phantom appeared at the start of 2003, the company only ever talked of annual sales of 1,000. The reduction merely reflected the reality of the market. New models in any segment tend to stimulate overall sales, so the almost simultaneous arrival of all-new models bearing the Rolls-Royce, Bentley and Maybach names around 2003 was certain to drive up demand. But not by as much as BMW, Volkswagen and Mercedes-Benz perhaps first thought. Each of them toned down its sales forecast as its product launch drew closer.

One questioner at the press conference wanted to know whether Morris would report to Piëch or Pischetsrieder. "He's mine. He used to work for me (at Audi) and I lost him." declared Piëch. "He used to work for me as well (at Rover) and I also lost him," Pischetsrieder retorted. What neither of them knew, though, was that Morris was coming to the conclusion he could not work for either of them. Kept in the dark about the decision to split Rolls-Royce and Bentley, he confidently reassured employees that the two would remain together. How could the workforce trust him again? Besides, everyone knew all the decisions would be made in Wolfsburg, not Crewe. Morris, they would say on the shop floor, was irrelevant.

Morris returned to Wolfsburg on the Volkswagen Falcon with the Volkswagen and BMW parties. He had an appointment that afternoon to present the 1999-2004 strategy for Rolls-Royce and Bentley to the group's executive committee. Curiously, in spite of Volkswagen having just ceded one of the brands to BMW, the presentation went ahead as planned. It made little sense in the light of what had happened. Morris returned to Cheshire that evening. Troubled by questions of credibility and integrity, he discussed the matter with his wife and a couple of his closest friends. He resolved not to make a decision through inactivity.

The following day, he phoned Piëch about his dilemma. Morris had tremendous respect for the achievements of the Volkswagen group and its chairman, but felt he had to resign because he had been put in an untenable position. It was a matter of principle: he told the people who worked at Crewe that the two companies would remain together, but developments that week meant he was unable to keep that promise. Piëch asked Morris to reconsider, which effectively meant another sleepless night. When they spoke again the following day, Morris confirmed his earlier decision to leave. He agreed to stay on until Christmas to help the personnel department select his replacement. The person appointed was the engineer who had been in charge of the development of the Silver Seraph and Arnage, Tony Gott. He, too, would be gone less than three years later.

For the employees at Crewe, Morris's action made him the honourable good guy. The latent resentment within the company concerned the split and the role in it played by Robins of Rolls-Royce plc. After the helter-skelter experience of private ownership and control by Vickers, employees recognised that the future of Rolls-Royce and Bentley would be more secure inside a large vehicle group. The nature of the car business by the late 20th century dictated that group would not be British. What the people at Crewe had trouble coming to terms with was that Rolls-Royce plc, a separate company which by an historical quirk happened to have the same name, should have such control over their destiny. Some Rolls-Royce Motors veterans thought Robins was in no position to make a qualitative judgements in the auto industry, and that Volkswagen ownership would have been a better outcome. The argument was that Volkswagen would have made far greater use of the twin brands of Rolls-Royce and Bentley because it had a much bigger hole at the top of its range. After all, the technical, commercial and marketing alliance between Rolls-Royce and Bentley had worked well enough for 70 years. With an existing presence in the luxury saloon market – the 7-series – the only clear role for the Rolls-Royce badge within BMW was on the front of a low-volume Phantom VI-style of car.

Effectively, Robins decided that BMW was the appropriate custodian of Rolls-Royce standards and Volkswagen was not. The stance was patently not true from an automotive perspective. Rather, it was shaped entirely by the *real politick* of the BR700 series turbofan aircraft engine. The joint venture between BMW and Rolls-Royce plc was not a great commercial success, though it was regarded as a technical success. In October the following year, it was revealed that BMW-Rolls-Royce GmbH would be turned into a wholly owned subsidiary of Rolls-Royce plc. In exchange, BMW became the largest industrial shareholder in Rolls-Royce plc with a stake of just over 10 per cent.

As the reality of the unique Rolls-Royce and Bentley car division began to sink in, though, time was running short for Pischetsrieder, Robins's old ally at BMW. Rover, the British group Pischetsrieder bought for BMW in early 1994, was living up to its name; it was an old dog. The historical problems of Rover's lack of investment, poor productivity and indifferent quality were compounded when the value of sterling began to rise. Exporting, one of the cornerstones of BMW's strategy for Rover, was made much more difficult. Rover's drain on BMW's performance became so great that it was nicknamed the English Patient after the popular film of the time.

The showdown with BMW's leading shareholders came in February 1999, a mere six months after Pischetsrieder's triumph with Rolls-Royce. Differences over how to cure the English Patient meant the chairman forfeited his job. So did Dr Wolfgang Reitzle, the board member responsible for R&D and Pischetsrieder's most obvious successor, because he failed to obtain a full endorsement from the supervisory board. In their place came Prof Joachim Milberg, a relative newcomer to BMW from the world of academia.

It was by no means the end of the Rover episode. When BMW decided in March 2000 to sell most of its Rover assets, three more board members resigned in protest. They included the man originally delegated by BMW to mastermind what became known as Project Rolls-Royce, Carl-Peter Forster. A former project leader for BMW's 5-series, Forster was later to emerge as chairman of General Motors' troubled Adam Opel subsidiary in Germany. For BMW, a group that had evolved so successfully, smoothly and conservatively over the previous two decades, the events after the acquisition of Rolls-Royce constituted an unprecedented maelstrom. With the exception of the unfortunate Forster, though, Project Rolls-Royce was too small to feel the blast. By the time the new Rolls-Royce was a production reality, BMW was back in the fast lane once more.

CHAPTER 22

THE KING IS DEAD. LONG LIVE THE KING

I n one respect, the separation of Rolls-Royce and Bentley put in place for 2003 would turn the calendar back to the 1920s. After seven decades of an often uneasy cohabitation it was difficult to comprehend that Rolls-Royce and Bentley were once more to be rivals for the attentions of the world's wealthiest car buyers. Another four and a half years living under the same roof, and the cars being sold through the same dealers, merely served to cloud the issue as far as the market was concerned.

Volkswagen, as temporary custodian of the Rolls-Royce flame, was naturally more preoccupied with the company whose long-term destiny it did control: Bentley. It did not ignore Rolls-Royce entirely. A more refined Silver Seraph was introduced in the autumn of 1999, a Corniche convertible the following January, and a long wheelbase Park Ward edition of the Silver Seraph a few weeks later. None of this could disguise the fact that demand for Rolls-Royces was in decline. Sales dropped by almost 30 per cent to 429 in the year after the split was announced. In no subsequent year under Volkswagen did they rise above 500. Tellingly, that was half the annual level that BMW projected for the model it was due to launch in January 2003.

In October 1998, Robert Büchelhofer, then the Volkswagen group's top sales and marketing man, revealed to Rolls-Royce and Bentley dealers that the parent group planned to invest £500 million in the two companies in the five years to 2003. By the standards of Crewe and Rolls-Royce, it was a dizzying figure. After all, the Silver Seraph and Arnage were brought to market for less than a third of that sum. The Continental R coupé based on the Turbo R of the early 1990s was brought to market for a trifling £19 million. However, Volkswagen's acknowledged investment was nowhere near the £1.5 billion it said it would put into Rolls-Royce and Bentley as part of the strategy to beat BMW.

Losing the responsibility for Rolls-Royce after 2002 would obviously scale back the requirement for quite so much Volkswagen investment. Similarly, when Büchelhofer spoke of eventually lifting annual sales to 9,000 – compared with the earlier figure of 10,000 – it reflected the scheduled departure of Rolls-Royce. Nevertheless, Bentley is certain to suck a great deal more than £500 million out of Volkswagen's coffers as the years unfold. The initial tranche was enough to upgrade the Crewe plant and to bring the Continental GT to market by the second half of 2003. It was not enough to launch the four-door saloon and two convertible versions of the Continental that are part of the product plan, or the replacement for the 1998 Arnage, or any other niche models.

Bentley's immediate product priority after the split was to do something about the unpopular BMW-powered Arnage. The model known as the Green Label remained in production only 18 months before it was replaced in the autumn of 1999 by the Red Label. Following an intensive engineering programme, the newcomer was powered by a turbocharged version of the company's traditional 6.75-litre V8. The engine, once confined to history, was extensively reworked to comply with emissions regulations. The important aspect for customers, though, was that the Red Label had about 15 per cent more power than the Green Label, and a massive 46 per cent more torque. It was an appropriately high-performance model properly reflecting the Bentley heritage.

When Graham Morris decided the brand split meant he could no longer remain as chief executive, Tony Gott, the company's engineering director, was quickly appointed acting chief executive. He was confirmed in the post in May 1999, at roughly the time Adrian Hallmark was appointed as board member for sales and marketing. Hallmark was well versed in the business of expensive cars, having previously been managing director of Porsche's British import company. The appointments were part of sweeping changes of top and second level management at the company increasingly identified as Bentley Motors. Dr Ulrich Hackenberg, the director of car body development at the Volkswagen brand, became Bentley's board member for engineering in May. Hans-Georg Melching, the finance specialist who was parachuted into Bentley as soon as Volkswagen took over, became full time board member for finance in July 1999. Doug Dickson, the board member responsible for manufacturing, joined at the start of 1999, having previously been managing director of BMW's Oxford factory where the Rover 75 was manufactured. The one survivor from the old Vickers days was Christine Gaskell, the board member for personnel. Bentley made another critical appointment in Dirk van Braeckel, who became director of styling and design. Van Braeckel, a Belgian graduate of London's Royal College of Art, was credited with creating the new face of Volkswagen's Skoda brand. He joined Bentley in April 1999, just as the newly commissioned Styling and Design Centre became operational.

Employees at Crewe felt the German influence in another way in December 1998, when they agreed to a system in which annual working hours were "banked" in periods of low demand, ready to be used when higher sales required additional labour. Though rare in Britain at the time, flexible working systems of this type successfully helped German car makers to remain competitive in periods of fluctuating demand.

The first two years after Rolls-Royce and Bentley changed hands was another difficult period for Crewe. There were new owners, new managers and new working practices. Soon, the old place would cease to be "Royce's", as its future as Bentley was being mapped out in secret. Employees knew about the astonishingly ambitious plan to expand the business. It meant they would be expected to produce three times more cars each year than Crewe had ever done. They did not know how it would be achieved. Besides, sales were static at around 1,500 a year, which was a sixth of the output Volkswagen was contemplating. Morale was low. Staff at Crewe, having been through the wringer several times over the years, did not know whether they would be able to send their children to university, commit to a house extension, or confidently book a holiday. The basic question everyone wanted answered was, will I have a job next year?

Tony Gott and Christine Gaskell decided to address those concerns with a bold plan. Bentley would lay bare its secret strategy to all employees. It clearly carried commercial dangers if employees talked openly about it to friends and colleagues who might pass on the information to competitors. There was also the risk of the media finding out.

In the late summer of 2000, one of Crewe's disused buildings was appropriated for a series of staff presentations. Gott, Hallmark and Dickson reminded each group of Bentley's early history, the acquisition by Rolls-Royce, the post-war Bentley boom, the near-death experience of the 1970s and the revival of more recent years. They went through the details of the investment programme, how it would affect Crewe's manufacturing structure, and why it was so important for the future. Just as importantly, they outlined Bentley's coming model programme. To make it more tangible, they displayed full-sized prototypes of two of them, the Arnage T to be launched in early 2002 and the all-important Continental GT that would form the company's cornerstone in the first decade of the new century. There was also a two-fifths scale model of a racing car that would mark Bentley's return to Le Mans the following year, even though the programme was not yet formally signed off. The 24-hours endurance race in France was the scene of Bentley's glory days, when it won the race five times in eight starts, a record that stood for many years.

The decision to take employees into the management's confidence proved a turning point. To the relief of all, and surprise of many, none of the details of the all-important Bentley strategy became public knowledge following the staff meetings. It perhaps reflected that what people had learned was positive news of a type that no one at Crewe could recall. Loyalty was warranted along with the possibility of university for the children, the house extension and the holiday. In November that year, Bentley officially confirmed that it would return to Le Mans for three consecutive years, starting in 2001. Volkswagen also introduced another feature that helped to rebuild morale. All employees were eligible to take part in a car-leasing programme. The rates were very attractive and all lease cars were replaced every nine months. Shiny new Golfs and Boras began to replace tired secondhand Ford Mondeos and Nissan Primeras in the company car parks.

The same summer, it was revealed Queen Elizabeth II was to be presented with a new state limousine by Britain's motor industry to mark her Golden Jubilee in 2002. The real surprise was, for the first time, the monarch's official car would be a Bentley. The queen had relied on a series of Rolls-Royce Phantoms for formal occasions after ascending the throne in 1952, though her father and grandfather always favoured Daimlers. Now, in another departure from tradition, she was to receive a car designed, developed and built by Bentley in association with 20 other motor industry contractors.

The Bentley state limousine was indicative of the revolution at Crewe. The famous old name on the front of the building in Pyms Road might be about to disappear, but Bentley's huge investment in new models and higher volumes, together with an ambitious motor sports programme, suggested a company with a very sound future.

Just over a year later, on September 11, 2001, it did not look that way. The spectacular terrorist attacks on New York and Washington prompted universal reappraisals of geopolitical and economic expectations. Vehicle makers suddenly looked vulnerable. There was no shortage of potential buyers, wealthy or otherwise, but security doubts began to surface about whether it was appropriate to be seen in a high-profile prestige model epitomising what was seen by some as a decadent western society.

An indication of the fall-out from those attacks came when Rolls-Royce and Bentley were obliged to move to a three-day working week. Orders from the United States crashed 60 per cent. While there was a subsequent recovery, sales of Bentleys the following year were still down 20 per cent. Not all was because of the terrorist threat. Buyers were increasingly aware of interesting developments likely in the market over the next couple of years. There was the proposed new-generation Bentley scheduled for the second half of 2003, the all-new Maybach in late 2002 and the equally new Rolls-Royce from BMW in early 2003. With the prospect of real choice in the luxury limousine sector for the first time in decades, the Arnage and Silver Seraph began to look old hat. Rolls-Royce sales fell 28 per cent in its run-out year at Crewe.

Two months after the trauma of 9/11, Crewe was subject to a more direct surprise. It was announced that Tony Gott, the chief executive for the previous three years and an employee at Crewe since 1984, was to leave "by mutual consent to pursue new challenges". While Gott emerged four months later as chief executive of BMW's Project Rolls-Royce in Goodwood, it is not entirely clear why he left the company where he worked for 17 years. He said in early 2003 he was certain Bentley's short- and medium-term futures were "in the bag" with the Continental GT series. His reservations appeared to centre on the Volkswagen aims for Bentley's longer term, which are not public knowledge. "At the top, you need to be *absolutely* committed to a path. Unless you are, you cannot take your colleagues with you," he said enigmatically.

Gott's departure gave Volkswagen the opportunity to put one of its trusted long-time managers into Bentley as chief executive. Dr Franz-Josef Paefgen, an engineer, started with Ford in Germany and joined Audi in 1980. He achieved Audi board of management status in 1995 and became its chairman in 1998. When he joined Bentley in March 2002, he was also head of the Volkswagen group's R&D department and responsible for its motor sports activities.

That meant Paefgen's old firm was his new firm's stiffest competitor in the Le Mans 24-hours race. While Audi's R8 models recorded an impressive hat-trick of wins in 2000-02, Team Bentley was consistently the best of the rest in the years it did race at Le Mans. A Bentley EXP Speed 8 achieved a very creditable third place in its debut year (2001) and fourth the following year. Then there was triumph in the all-important 2003 event, the third and final year to which Team Bentley was committed. The Speed 8s of Guy Smith/Tom Kristensen/Dindo Capello and Mark Blundell/David Brabham/Johnny Herbert pulled off a convincing Bentley one-two. It was the firm's sixth Le Mans win, and its first in 73 years. An elated Paefgen declared it was "one of the greatest moments in our company's long history". From every perspective, the risky racing strategy paid off to provide the perfect platform for the sales launch of the Continental GT a few months later.

Back at Crewe, an era ended with hardly anyone outside the factory gates noticing. The last Rolls-Royce under the old regime rolled off the production line at the end of August 2002. The car, a silver Corniche convertible normally sold for £250,000, was retained for the company's museum. Crewe, created to make Rolls-Royce aircraft engines, produced a total of 70,977 Rolls-Royce cars between 1946 and 2002. Now its future was to be wholly identified with Bentley. A couple of weeks later, Bentley Motor Cars was renamed Bentley Motors, the name favoured by the founder of the company. At that autumn's Paris motor show, where the new Continental GT made its world debut, Rolls-Royce was absent for the first time in its history.

At the heart of Bentley's future was the series initially known as the MSB, or Medium-Sized Bentley. The Continental GT, the first of the series, is less expensive than other models in the Bentley range, but definitely not cheap. A pre-tax launch price of £110,000 was announced, which made the model around 15 per cent less than the Arnage R saloon and 35 per cent below the price of the Continental R. When the Continental line-up is complemented by the saloon and convertible versions, the series is expected to constitute around 80 per cent of all Bentley sales.

In spite of the code name, the Continental GT making its public debut in September 2002 was anything but mid-sized. It turned out to be a very large two-door coupé indeed, getting on for the length of the four-door Arnage. The first sight confirmed that Dirk van Braeckel and his design colleagues had drawn their inspiration from the Continental R of the 1950s and the big racing Bentleys of the 1920s. The moody black and white publicity material accompanying the launch aimed to reinforce a more glamorous facet of a bygone era.

If the Continental GT looked the part – taut, muscular and athletic – and carried the promise of an appropriately high performance, it was technically unlike any Bentley that came before. The company's engineers were able to draw on the Volkswagen group's impressive technology resources to produce a 6-litre double-vee engine of the type usually referred to in English as a W. In the Volkswagen/Bentley case, the engine comprised two 15 degree 3-litre V6s splayed at an angle of 72 degrees and with a common crankshaft. Even when equipped with twin turbochargers, the result was a relatively compact unit delivering a spectacular 552 horsepower and an even more astonishing 650 Nm of torque at only 1,600 rpm. An easily believable top speed in excess of 190 mph was claimed.

But if the style and high performance were throwbacks to Bentley's heritage, everything mechanical was thoroughly German. The engines are assembled at Crewe, but from imported components. All major mechanical items, including the gearbox, four-wheel-drive system, steering, brakes, suspension and general chassis construction are derived from other Volkswagen group products. Most are imported as ready-to-install units from Germany, including painted body-in-white units from Volkswagen's factory in Mosel. A senior Volkswagen engineer jubilantly exclaimed during the Continental GT's development stage, "Just imagine! We can sell a Phaeton for another $60,000!"

The value-added in Crewe comes in the beautiful wood, leather and carpet trim, the engine assembly, and the final car assembly. Bentley likes to think of its contribution as manufacturing, but it requires a leap of faith to accept that argument. The new range has nothing like the depth of local production that Porsche achieves in Stuttgart or Ferrari in Maranello – or Bentley or Rolls-Royce two or three decades earlier, when Crewe even made its own nuts and bolts. Indeed, nice "Japanese" saloons made by Nissan, Honda and Toyota in

Britain have a higher British content than a modern Bentley that is promoted internationally as a traditional English car. As we will see, the manufacturing structure at the new Rolls-Royce assembly plant near Goodwood paints an even more Made-in-Germany picture.

CHAPTER 23

BMW BUILDS A ROLLS-ROYCE

W hen the drama of the 1998 marque separation was over, BMW had bought the right to make and sell cars with the Rolls-Royce name on them from the start of 2003. It would be able to decorate the radiator shells of those cars with the symbolic Spirit of Ecstasy statue, and to give the cars names from Rolls-Royce's history, thanks to the agreement negotiated between Bernd Pischetsrieder of BMW and Ferdinand Piëch of Volkswagen. And that is all BMW got. When the Phantom was launched in January 2003, it was an all-new car from an all-new company with a 99-year-old name. The episode was unique in the history of the car industry.

BMW decided to create a miniature, stand-alone car maker, which meant it had just under four and a half years to complete a Rolls-Royce turnkey operation. The only investment the group acknowledges in the project is £40 million to acquire the rights to the Rolls-Royce name and £60 million to build a new home and final assembly plant for it in England. What it cost in terms of product development is anyone's guess. In spite of being able to draw on the group resources, it is probably such a huge sum that BMW does not wish the world to know its precise size. DaimlerChrysler is equally coy about the investment involved in resurrecting Maybach Manufaktur.

Referred to as Project Rolls-Royce during the transition period, it officially became Rolls-Royce Motor Cars on January 1, 2003. By then the company had established its own departments for design, engineering, purchasing, production, sales and marketing, finance and personnel. To make sure everything was ready for business when the transfer date arrived, the project team therefore had to design and engineer a wholly new model, find a site for an assembly plant, construct it, recruit a workforce, sign supplier agreements and establish a global dealer network. The task of directing Project Rolls-Royce was assigned to Karl-Heinz Kalbfell, the BMW group's senior vice president for marketing. He co-ordinated the endeavour until the arrival in March 2002 of Tony Gott, the engineer who earlier quit the Volkswagen-owned Bentley and Rolls-Royce business to "pursue new challenges".

The first few months after the split were spent defining the project. For BMW, the challenge was to understand what made the difference between a grandiose Rolls-Royce and other top-level luxury saloons. Team members analysed and drove all competitors' cars, but the process was rather like working in the dark. While BMW knew plenty of wealthy customers through sales of its top-line 7-series saloon, 8-series coupé and forthcoming Z8 roadster, it had no direct experience of the expectations of buyers in the segment of the market occupied by Rolls-Royce. Neither did it have access to a database of past or current Rolls-Royce owners, because that remained the property of the Volkswagen-owned firm in Crewe.

When planning the new model, though, members of the Project Rolls-Royce team knew they could virtually ignore the content and engineering of most Rolls-Royce models of the previous quarter of a century. These were products of financial restraints during a period when the way in which cars were designed and manufactured was transformed by electronics and new ideas about technology and engineering. Old Rolls-Royce thinking would be irrelevant in the early 21st century because the company had missed two or three generations of new models. At least this meant the project team could safely start without lots of preconceptions.

The priority was to get the design and engineering of the 2003 model under way. The design team, personally selected by BMW design director Chris Bangle, was led by Ian Cameron, a Briton who was previously responsible for the exterior of the BMW 3-series. In February 1999, he and a small team moved into temporary studios on London's Bayswater Road, located in a converted former Westminster Bank branch that was soon known internally as The Bank. The location was a good one as The Bank was a brief drive from some of London's wealthiest areas – Mayfair, Knightsbridge, Chelsea, Kensington and Holland Park. This was archetypal Rolls-Royce territory, allowing the designers to absorb at close quarters the lifestyles associated with ownership of such a prestigious car.

Meanwhile, a Project Rolls-Royce engineering team, for what was known at that stage as RR01, was established in Munich under Dr Tim Leverton. It was not located within BMW's giant FIZ engineering centre, but about 10 minutes away in a separate building in Heidemann Strasse with its own dedicated staff. "That 10-minute drive was an important psychological factor," reported Leverton, who became the project's first engineering recruit in April 1999 when he transferred from Land Rover, at that point still a BMW group company.

While the Project Rolls-Royce designers and engineers were wholly absorbed by the minutiae of their planning, the wider world of the BMW group went through a period of unprecedented turbulence. Differences of opinion concerning the strategy for the troublesome Rover group led to the departures in February 1999 of Bernd Pischetsrieder – the architect of the Rover and Rolls-Royce purchases – and of the group's top engineer, Wolfgang Reitzle. Thirteen months later, in March 2000, BMW board members Carl-Peter Forster, Dr Heinrich Heitmann and Dr Wolfgang Ziebart became victims of the Rover controversy as well. The controversial MG Rover and Land Rover sell-offs left the BMW group with only two other brands: Mini, which was scheduled for a July 2001 launch, and Rolls-Royce. Between them, the trio of brands was destined to form a portfolio of models retailing from under £9,000 to over £200,000 before tax.

The designers provided plenty of ideas for the new Rolls-Royce.

However, clay models would be needed before the exterior design of the RR01 could be signed off. In May 1999, the project's focus moved across London from The Bank to The Bookshop, a former film studio in Holborn, where six clay models of two-fifths scale were produced. The version finally selected for production that December was by Marek Djordjevic, a Croatian who previously worked for BMW's Designworks studios in California.

The formula Project Rolls-Royce settled on for RR01 revolved around an aluminium space frame chassis, a 6.75-litre version of the group's V12 engine, and a six-speed automatic transmission sourced from ZF. The emphasis was on refinement, silence and effortless performance, or what Rolls-Royce identified as "waftability". The V12 engine was tuned to produce 452 horsepower and a massive pulling power of 720 Nm at 3,500 rpm. However, 75 per cent of that peak torque was available from only 1,000 rpm – little more than the engine idle speed. Top speed would be restricted to 149 mph.

The first impression of the car when it was finally revealed was one of sheer scale. Taller than a Jeep Cherokee, as wide as a Cadillac Escalade and longer than a Lincoln Navigator, the Phantom is so large that it makes a BMW 7-series look like a 3-series by comparison. Visually, it contains echoes of the Phantoms of the 1930s and the Silver Clouds of the post-war era thanks to the very long bonnet, huge wheels and short overhangs at the front and rear. The rearwards-opening rear doors and high floor were adopted for an elegant exit when the palace footman opens the door.

The Phantom's appearance has the defiant stance of a bulldog. It is an unapologetic rejection of the design trend requiring a modern car to look as slippery as used soap. It is a vertical opposite to the long, low look created by DaimlerChrysler for the Maybach, its chief rival. The look is a coded message to would-be buyers about power, wealth, confidence and influence.

The realisation that BMW intended to have Rolls-Royces made in England sent a frisson of anticipation through local development corporations across the country. Numerous applications to host the factory poured in. Each had to be seriously considered. By the spring of 2000, members of the Project Rolls-Royce team had whittled the list down to five candidates. Its choice, made in May that year, surprised everyone.

The Earl of March's Goodwood estate around Chichester in southern England was not an obvious place for a car factory. Nestling in the South Downs, Goodwood is a picture-perfect area of honey-coloured houses and rolling hills. The region, which has no tradition of manufacturing, is a world apart from the gritty, red-brick industrial town 230 miles to the north that was home to Rolls-Royce for half a century. Or, indeed, Derby or Manchester where the cars were made in the first half of the century.

When the site was selected, great emphasis was placed on the quality of the transport infrastructure. In addition to being reasonably close to Gatwick and Heathrow airports, Goodwood, a former Royal Air Force airfield, still has facilities for light aircraft. Rolls-Royce thought the region's cultural and sporting events would also appeal to a buyer visiting the factory to collect a car. Events include the Chichester Arts Festival, horse racing at Goodwood, and the popular Festival of Speed and motor racing revival meeting at the renovated Goodwood race track. The nearby Solent estuary is the country's premier yachting area, and home to the world-famous Cowes Week. If all these seemed like tenuous reasons for deciding the location of the new enterprise, the symbolism that appealed most to the Project Rolls-Royce team was that from 1917 until his death in 1933, Sir Henry Royce lived at West Wittering, about 10 miles from Goodwood. For some reason, Royce's formative years living near Peterborough, Leeds, Liverpool and Manchester seemed to hold less appeal to the decision-makers than Goodwood.

Formal planning permission for the Goodwood development was lodged in November 2000. Despite the prestigious nature of the project and the prospect of the additional jobs it would bring, the proposal raised some local opposition because of the region's unspoiled rural nature. However, in May the following year, Chichester District Council overwhelmingly approved the project. The race was then on to develop the site for the start of production

17 months later.

The brief given to Nicholas Grimshaw and Partners, the architectural practice awarded the contract, was for an environmentally sound development. It also had to blend with the surrounding countryside, which was rather different from one of the practice's earlier commissions to design the Eden Project, the giant biosphere now a huge tourist attraction in Cornwall.

The Goodwood site already had planning permission for gravel extraction, so that went ahead and the new buildings were constructed partially below ground. The shape of the buildings, covering about 20 per cent of the 17 hectare site, was planned to follow the natural contours of the landscape. They were designed around a central courtyard, approached by a bridge over a lake, and surrounded by extensive landscaping. The roof of the low-rise main building was planted with thousands of sedum, which change colour with the seasons, to create Europe's largest "living roof". The biomass adds to the insulation by cutting down heat loss. Approximately 400,000 trees and shrubs were planted in the grounds to help the buildings blend with the surroundings.

The office and assembly complex was designed for energy efficiency. The lakes that are part of the landscape form a vital part of the drainage system for the site. They are also the means by which the air supply for the building is cooled. Air is pumped through heat-exchangers in the lakes and then circulated to the buildings instead of using conventional, electrically powered air conditioning. As a result, the main offices use about one-fifth of the energy of an equivalent air-conditioned office, and the assembly building about one-third of an equivalent facility. Lighting costs were reduced by the use of huge glass walls running the length of the assembly area. A computer-controlled louvre system automatically adjusts the amount of light entering the buildings depending on the strength and angle of the sun.

The Goodwood headquarters is an echo of the product made inside. It is to most car factories what a stately home is to a suburban house. It is easy to forget that the purpose of this modern working monument to architecture and the environment is to make cars. But not too many of them, because supply must always run one behind demand in order to maintain the Rolls-Royce mystique. The company talks of selling an average of 1,000 cars a year over the Phantom's life cycle of 10 to 12 years. As each car is said to contain up to 2,600 hours of labour, that suggests Rolls-Royce requires nearly 2.6 million hours of labour a year to turn out its thousand cars. It is an astonishing level, way beyond the capacity of Rolls-Royce's 350 employees at Goodwood to supply. Even with overtime, they could not contribute more than 700,000 hours a year between them.

The answer, of course, is that Goodwood assembles a vehicle largely manufactured in Germany, which is where it was mainly engineered in the first place. The space frame chassis and bodywork are fabricated in BMW's Dingolfing factory, the engines come from the group's Munich plant, and the transmission is from ZF, another German supplier. All other major mechanical and electronic components are also imported. Goodwood's role is to paint the bodies in what the company ostentatiously calls the Surface Technology Centre, to hand-craft the beautiful wood and leather trim, and to carry out final assembly. The wood and leather are imported, as is most of the machinery to work them.

There is another irony. Goodwood employees are provided with work clothing that apes the tweed, Viyella and corduroy attire of the English country gentleman. It is very smart, high-quality clothing with covered buttons which cannot scratch a car's paintwork. The jacket lining proudly declares "Rolls-Royce". It also contains a label that reads "Made in Germany". The clothing example epitomises BMW's philosophy over Rolls-Royce. Despite appearances to the contrary, the content of this archetypal upper-crust English limousine is overwhelmingly German.

CHAPTER 24

WAS IT WORTH IT?

C ar exhibitions are the international vehicle industry equivalent of fashion's catwalk shows and the film world's famous
festivals. They are the fixed points in the calendar when the sector's
powerbrokers parade, to see and be seen. They are there to dispense
the benefit of their wisdom to the world and to exchange pleasantries
with their peers.

For the people who work in the automotive business, each year
begins with Detroit in early January, an inhospitable time to visit a
Mid-West industrial city. Two months later, the scene switches to
Geneva, serene and self-satisfied under the snow-capped Swiss Alps.
Europe remains the setting for the key exhibitions that alternate each
autumn: Paris, which everyone loves because it is Paris, and
Frankfurt, which everyone hates because its scale makes it so physically demanding. Every other year, there is about a month to recover
from the rigours of Frankfurt before it is time for the long haul to
Tokyo. There, the show is set in a sterile wasteland between Narita
airport and the bright lights of the Ginza. After that, it is time to start
planning for Detroit once more.

These show visits, with their new model introductions, cocktail
parties, fine food and five-star hotels, are the more glamorous face of
the car industry. They are far removed from the reality of endless
planning meetings, long hours in the test lab, the never-ending production line, or battles with suppliers over prices, delivery times and

quality. The launch of any new product at a car show represents the optimistic public persona of a complex, capital intensive, high-technology industry. If a company gets a new product right, it will generate steady cash for the next four to six years. If it gets it wrong, more than reputations and careers are at stake. The history of the motor industry is littered with examples of poor product decisions that gradually, inexorably, led to the demise of once-proud names. And the process is by no means over.

That was why the *Mondial de l'Automobile* in Paris in September 2002 and the North American International Auto Show in Detroit in January 2003 were so critical to the two English luxury car makers. The new Bentley and Rolls-Royce had to be right. At last, members of the public were able to judge whether a Bentley by Volkswagen and a Rolls-Royce by BMW were in keeping with the spirits of their early traditions. The extent of their different future directions was confirmed when the Continental GT was unveiled in Paris, followed a few weeks later by the Phantom in Detroit. They were as different as the work of Elton John and Edward Elgar. The Bentley looked muscular and athletic, perhaps a little *risqué*. The Rolls-Royce was dignified and imposing, an appropriate carriage for a head of state. After all the years of cohabitation, when radiator grilles were frequently the only distinction between the two, Rolls-Royce and Bentley had returned to their earlier, distinctive roots. Those inherent differences were belatedly recognised when Vickers owned both companies, but the irony is that it took two wealthy rival German firms to achieve the proper separation.

However, the story does not necessarily end happily there. The rest of the international motor industry questions whether all the money and manpower involved in their purchases and new product programmes were well spent. Scores of sceptics maintain that all the effort and money was to re-create a past era, a process driven more by egos than economics. Everyone recognises the benefits the halo effect of a prestige brand can have on a group as a whole, but there are deep reservations about the commercial credibility and wisdom of such enterprises.

There are fewer doubts about whether enough truly wealthy

customers exist to afford these mega-money cars, if they wish to. Recent evidence suggests they don't. The anecdotal evidence about the extent of great wealth can be seen in the number of private aircraft parked at a small regional airport like Stuttgart, or the armada of yachts filling the harbour at Monaco for the annual Grand Prix. Bentley says any one of its Arnage customers probably owns eight to ten other cars. Bankers Merrill Lynch and consultants Cap Gemini Ernst & Young get together each year to produce a more empirical study of the world's wealthy. The authors believe there are more than 7 million people with investable assets (not including property) of more than $1 million. And there are nearly 60,000 with investable assets of at least $30 million.

That would certainly seem sufficient to support the sale of a few thousand limousines each year. Rolls-Royce and Maybach each projects annual sales of 1,000, and Bentley, with its cheaper entry level models, talks in terms of 9,000 a year. On the face of it, their sales targets look easily achievable. It requires only one in under 700 of those $1 million-plus people to support all three enterprises each year.

But recent evidence suggests the world's wealthy are not that bothered about owning such grand vehicles. In 2002, before the new Maybach had any real impact on the market, Rolls-Royce and Bentley dominated the limousine sector. Their combined sales of just under 1,400 cars that year was not an aberration. In the decade leading up to the separation of Rolls-Royce and Bentley, their combined average annual sales amounted to 1,600. However that had to be set against an annual average sale of just under 2,500 achieved in the previous 10 years.

It constituted a major shift in buying patterns. The sector is now expected to undergo a total transformation in the opposite direction. While this premium limousine market contracted by more than a third over the past decade, Rolls-Royce, Bentley and Maybach are collectively banking on their new models to lead to a seven-fold increase in business over the coming decade. It hardly seems possible. While there was a great deal of initial buyer interest in the new models, no one knows whether the sales expectations are sustainable over the long term.

So what are the world's wealthiest individuals buying? They are obviously buying more long wheelbase, top-specification Mercedes-Benz S-class and BMW 7-series then ever. In itself this represents a failure by Rolls-Royce and Bentley, and by the companies that controlled their purse strings over the years. A part of the market, once exclusively theirs, has been progressively eroded by cars that had an inferior social status but were technologically superior.

However, in contrast to the slumping fortunes of Rolls-Royce and Bentley, demand for exceedingly expensive high-performance roadsters and coupés was at record levels in the early 21st century. Porsche, Ferrari and Ford-owned Aston Martin were never more popular. There were big expansion plans for Audi's Lamborghini subsidiary and for Maserati, which is now part of the Ferrari stable. The performance and price threshold were pushed even higher in 2003, when Porsche launched its Carrera GT and Mercedes-Benz its McLaren-built SLR. Each car costs as much as a Phantom or a Maybach. And then there was Volkswagen's scheme to offer the world a model it did not even realise it needed, the 1,000-horsepower Bugatti Veyron.

So, a comparison of sales returns makes it difficult to escape the conclusion that the visceral thrills of the truly high-performance sports car have gained at the expense of the cosseted comfort provided by stately limousines. Perhaps it says something about the age in which we live: the Ferrari is for the ambitious and aggressive young Master of the Universe, the Rolls-Royce more fitting for a fading earl a bit down on his luck. Only time will tell whether the shift away from limousines is permanent. If it is, the business cases for Rolls-Royce, Bentley and Maybach will begin to look increasingly wobbly. Few rival car makers thought they looked very stable in the first place, although Volkswagen's Bernd Pischetsrieder insisted Bentley would be profitable in 2004 on anticipated sales volumes of 5,000. His optimism even began to look attainable at the Geneva motor show in March 2003, when Bentley said it had received 3,200 orders for the Continental GT, which was due to go on sale in the second half of that year.

This development of the limousine sector certainly involved a great deal of money and effort being lavished on very few cars. Volkswagen, for example, devoted vast amounts of management time to the Bentley acquisition. It also handed over handsome sums for financial advice from Morgan Stanley, although the bank's assignments from Volkswagen subsequently dried up. Vickers received nearly £480 million from Volkswagen for what in the end was only Bentley, which then required an additional £500 million for factory improvements and a new line of vehicles. Volkswagen will have to spend yet more to complete the Bentley model renewal programme.

BMW bought the Rolls-Royce rights for £40 million and then invested £60 million in the Goodwood headquarters and assembly plant. The amount of money involved in the development of the Phantom was never revealed. Similarly, Mercedes-Benz declined to make public its investment in the resurrection of the Maybach. Nevertheless, to get the Phantom and Maybach to market probably set each maker back half a billion pounds. In the case of the Rolls-Royce, however, the flexibility of its aluminium space frame construction means that model variations, and even a second generation of cars a decade later, can be launched at comparatively little cost.

All of that investment was to sell 9,000 Bentleys a year at pre-tax prices starting at £110,000, and a combined total of 2,000 Rolls-Royces and Maybachs at around £250,000 each.

Even if the cars meet their long-term sales objectives, the world cannot assess whether these exercises were worthwhile unless the companies are prepared to be more transparent about their finances. There is no indication they will be. Is the business of making prestigious limousines a financially sound operation in the early 21st century, or is ownership primarily an enhancement of a group's image? The answer is subject to obfuscation. Specific research and development costs, for example, can be buried within a group's general R&D budget. And in the cases of Volkswagen and BMW, the costs involved in running Bentley and Rolls-Royce can be used as tax offsets on profits made by subsidiary companies that import their mainstream brands into Britain. Car makers have traditionally enjoyed higher profit margins on cars sold in Britain than in the rest of western Europe. And the advantage of selling cars in Britain sourced from the euro zone was boosted by the strength of sterling at the start of the decade, the very period when the big investments in Bentley and Rolls-Royce took place. Tax credits would be very handy under the circumstances.

The absence of reliable financial data requires some assumptions on the part of any outsider trying to understand the business. In the Volkswagen example – the only one for which there are at least some financial guidelines – its acknowledged £980 million involvement in Bentley will cost it around £59 million a year at the normal borrowing costs. It seems doubtful whether the group can cover that cost through Bentley sales. A good average achievement for a prestige car maker across the economic cycle is an operating margin of around 7 per cent. Perhaps a big ticket item like a Bentley will earn more. Even if that seems paltry in comparison with the margins involved in selling bottled water or posh frocks, it should be remembered that volume car makers do well to produce 2 or 3 per cent. That is why volume is so critical to a mass-market car manufacturer.

At 7 per cent on the target peak production volume of 9,000 cars a year, the Bentley return on Volkswagen's investment would be approximately £55 million a year. This is only a rough estimate, because some Bentleys already cost more than the Continental GT and some future models are expected to cost a little less. What is does indicate, though, is that consistently high sales numbers will be critical to meet the cost of borrowing. Can Bentley achieve those volumes when it never did historically? While the all-new model will be an excellent stimulus for potential customers, the equation is complicated by the assumptions on the part of Rolls-Royce and Maybach that they, too, will win a fair slice of the evolving limousine business. What we also know is that there are enough wealthy people who can afford to buy all three.

BMW paid a token sum for the use of the Rolls-Royce name,

while Mercedes-Benz already owned Maybach. But on the assumption that the investment required to develop their new cars was broadly similar to Volkswagen's for Bentley, the cost of their capital would run at around £30 million a year. Despite their lower anticipated volumes, their higher transfer prices would produce an operating income of around £11 million if 7 per cent margins are achieved. All of this, of course, is academic, because the companies will have written off the initial investments and count only operating costs in their profit and loss accounts.

To anyone born and brought up in Britain, or anyone who has a sense of the country's history and culture, the changes of Rolls-Royce and Bentley ownership are matters of great sadness. I am frequently asked by friends and neighbours whether this had to be their fate. Indeed, it still seems curious that marques created in the early 20th century as patriotic English responses to all the imported cars of the day are now owned by German firms. That, though, is the reality.

From the moment in 1997 when Vickers finally came to understand that the Rolls-Royce and Bentley sector was a cruel combination of enormous investments and unpredictable demand, and that there were limited synergies between main battle tanks and luxury limousines, it was inevitable that these two quintessentially English nameplates would end up under foreign ownership. Their disposals were part of a long, post-war cycle that saw the gradual decimation of Britain's indigenous motorcycle, car, truck, bus, tractor and component sectors. That is why the latest Rolls-Royces and Bentleys have so little local content: there are not enough British companies able to supply the high quality components and materials necessary for a car maker to be internationally competitive today.

In the car sector, the independent survivors in the late 1990s comprised a handful of privately owned sports car firms and a couple of taxi makers. MG Rover subsequently become independent once more when BMW gave the company to its management and employees, though its long-term future as a vehicle maker is in considerable doubt. Today, the car industry in Britain is under the control of various large American, Japanese, French and German vehicle makers. Funnily enough, it has not been as competitive in years.

In truth, the outcome of the Vickers decision to ditch Rolls-Royce and Bentley could never have been much different because of the structural flaws in British society. Over the years, an inadequate system of education and training, hopeless management, confrontational employees, government meddling and financial neglect by investors turned the country's industrial core into a wasteland. No other developed nation in the world squandered so much potential wealth-creation in so little time. It was not just bad luck on Britain's part. Other countries suffered their setbacks as well, but the wholesale nature of the decline in Britain's vehicle industries amounts to an indictment of the companies involved and the country that was their home. The places where car factories once furiously forged, cast, stamped and welded in order to turn metals into motor cars are now shopping centres selling this-and-thats made in sweat shops in developing nations.

The only realistic bidders when Rolls-Royce and Bentley went on the block were Volkswagen, BMW and Daimler-Benz. The effect of the sale was made clear less than five years later. The cars may still be assembled in Britain, but the centre of gravity in the ultimate limousine sector of the car market, for years the exclusive preserve of Britain, was simply transferred to Germany with the arrival of the trio's respective Bentley, Rolls-Royce and Maybach marques. What happened to Rolls-Royce and Bentley was a microcosm of the fate of Britain's vehicle-building business as a whole.

air-conditioning 114
aircraft engines 27–33, 54,
    57–9, 136
Alfa Romeo acquisition 83
America see USA
Arnage models 12, 16, 110,
    114
Aston Martin 71, 75, 77,
    119–20
Audi A8 86
Austin, Herbert 44

bankruptcy 67–79
Bentley 35, 43–9, 87, 89–97,
    102–3, 182–90
    Brunei bonanza 119, 121,
        122
    lifeline 115–23
    nameplate to Volkswagen
        177
    Project 90 96
Bentley Motors 165, 188
Bentley, Walter Owen 43–4,
    48
Bentley models
    Continental Type R
        89–90, 97, 115–16
    Eight saloon 95, 97
    Green/Red Label 183
    Java 109, 119, 121, 122,
        160
    Mk V 56
    Mk VI 63, 64, 89–90
    Mulsanne 94
    Speed 8 188
    T-series 71
    turbocharged 94, 95–6, 97
Benz 19, 37
BMW 7–9, 10–17, 75, 86,
    106–14, 191–7, 201
    bid by Mercedes-Benz 61
    car components 171
    car sales 1998 158
    Daimler-Benz takeover
        132
    North America 67
    post-war period 132
    Rover Group purchase
        151–2
    RR name 177
    RR plc 165, 171, 180
    Volkswagen discussions
        160–2, 164, 171–3
    X5 107
BP see Pischetsrieder, Bernd
Briggs, Arthur 24
Bristol cars 60–1
British Leyland 75, 83
Brunei 11–12, 115–23

Büchelhofer, Robert 182–3
Bugatti, Ettore 46, 174
Buzzard V12 41–2

Camargue 73, 78
car exhibitions 198–205
Chandler, Colin 107–8, 111,
    112–13, 150, 156, 163
chassis 31, 57
Citroen 76, 77
Claremont, Ernest 22
coach-building 56, 63–4, 91,
    102, 122
computer design 85
Conduit Street sale 126
Continental
    GT 183, 187–9
    R/S Types 49, 89–90, 97,
        115–16
Corniche 49, 73, 172, 182
Cosworth 8–9, 88, 124, 170
Crewe 58, 100–1, 144–5
    contraction 108
    major changes 124–9
    Merrill's Farm 57, 58
    move to 57
    production facilities 125
    production increase
        184–5
Crewe Motors 159
C.S. Rolls & Co. 20–1, 24

Daimler 19, 37
Daimler-Benz 104, 131, 134
DaimlerChrysler 104, 148, 191
David Brown 71, 75
Derby 25, 33, 48–9, 53
Dixi factory 131
D. Napier & Son 41, 47
double-R logo 172
Dunne, Mike 91–2, 110

Eagle aircraft engines 32, 38
EGM at Volkswagen 168–9
Eight saloon (Bentley) 95, 97
electronics 99, 109, 114

Feller, Fritz 84
Fenn, George 91
F.H. Royce & Co. 22
fighter aircraft 58–9, 68, 132
Ford 25, 40, 52, 74–5, 83
Fraser, Ian 73, 81
fuel injection 95, 99

gas turbine engines 60, 136
Goldfish (BMW) 111
Golf (Volkswagen) 77–8
Goodwood race track 195–7

Goshawk aircraft engine 35
Gott, Tony 110, 125, 128–9,
    183–4, 187
Great Arrow Car Company 38
Great War aftermath 34–42
Green/Red Label Bentleys 183
Griffon engines 59
Grylls, Harry 64, 66

Hanson, James 74
Hassanal Bolkiah of Brunei,
    Sultan 115–23
Hives, Ernest 53–5, 58

Jaguar 74–5, 83
Japan 86, 103, 106–7
Java (Bentley) 109, 119, 121,
    122, 160
Jefri, Prince (Brunei) 11–12,
    115–23, 146
jet propulsion 59
Johnson, C. 21, 24, 28–9, 37–8
just-in-time delivery systems
    125

Kocks, Klaus 172–3, 176
von Kuenheim, Eberhard 132,
    151

Lamborghini, Ferrucio 77
Land Rover 107
Lazard document 146, 147–8
Le Mans 45–6, 186–8
Liesen, Klaus 6–7
life cycles 84, 85
limousines 186, 200–2
Lockhead-L1011 69–70
Lüderitz, Hagen 167, 173

Maserati 77, 104
mass production 37
Maybach 135–6, 137
Mayflower 109–10, 137–8
Mercedes-Benz 87, 151
    bid for BMW 61
    Maybach 135–6, 137
    S-class 86, 134, 201
Merlin aero-engine 54, 58–9
Merrill's Farm, Crewe 57, 58
Mini project 17
Ministry of Defence 100
Model T Ford 30, 40
mono-culture corporations
    68
Montagu, John 25
Morris, Graham 15, 140–4,
    146, 169, 170, 175–6,
    178–9
Morris, William 44

motorcycles 131, 132
MRP2 process 100
MSB see medium size Bentley
MSBs 127–8, 142
MTU (Daimler-Benz) 112, 151
Mulsanne 80, 94

name ownership 159, 164, 166, 177
Nicholson, E.R. 71, 72–3, 75
Nissan 103, 104

P600 projects 126–7, 128
Park Ward 56, 63–4, 91, 102, 182
Paulin, Georges 49
Perry, Dick 91–2
Peugeot 19, 20, 76
Phantoms 36, 178
   III/IV/VI 50, 52–3, 55, 62–3, 121
Piëch, Ferdinand 6, 14–16, 150, 152, 153, 154–6
   secret negotiations 161–2, 171–3
   Volkswagen vision 133–4
Pischetsrieder, Bernd (BP) 7–10, 12–14, 16–17, 150–1, 152–3
   von Kuenheim's successor 132
   Robins agreement 165, 176–7
   secret negotiations 161–2, 171–3
   takeover strategy 108–9, 112–13, 114
Plastow, David 71–2, 73, 74, 81, 88, 90–1, 106–7
Porsch 153, 154, 155–6
post-War era 60–6
Pressed Steel... 64, 84
Project 90 96
Project Rolls-Royce 192–5
Purves, Tom 67

R engine 41–2
RB-211 turbo-fan engines 68–70, 71–2
receivers, Bentley 35
Red Flag Act 1865 18, 20
Reitzle, Wolfgang 107–8, 181
Renault 104
restructuring Rolls-Royce Motors 102–3
revival of Bentley 89–97
Robins, Ralph 9–10, 12–13, 15, 111–12, 150, 157,

180
Pischetsrieder agreement 165, 176–7
Rolls-Royce name 164–5
Rolls, Charles Stewart 18–26, 27, 28
Rolls-Royce 34–49, 51–2, 54–5, 57–9, 60–3, 67–79
   see also individual models
   aircraft engines 31–2, 34–42, 57–9
   Bali project 160
   Bentley separation 182–90
   built by BMW 191–7
   buying Bentley 43–9
   car sales 1978-82 82
   leaving Crewe 176
   lifeline 115–23
   merger with Vickers 81
   Ministry of Defence 100
   name rights 146
   possible buyers 107
   Spirit of Ecstacy use 171–2
   standards custodian 180
   as subsidiary 102–3
   Vickers sale idea 136
   world-wide sale recovery 126
Rolls-Royce (1971) Ltd. 71
Rolls-Royce Action Committee 147, 159
Rolls-Royce Motor Cars 131, 138–9, 140–9, 150–7, 158, 163–5, 171
Rolls-Royce Motors 9–10, 102–3
Rolls-Royce Motors Ltd. 72–4, 75, 76, 80–1, 87
Rolls-Royce plc 165, 171, 172, 180
   name ownership 159, 164, 166, 177
Rover Group 107, 151–2
Royce, Frederick Henry 18–26, 29–30, 48, 50–6
Royce, Minnie 30
`Royce's' 175, 184
RR01 see Project Rolls-Royce

S-class (Mercedes) 134–5
sales figures comparison 1998 158–9
Schneider Trophy 41–2, 54
Schröder, Helmut 6
seaplanes 41–2
SEAT 83, 104, 152
Shrimpton, Michael 159, 169

Sidgreaves, Arthur 53
Silver Clouds/Dawns 64–5
Silver Ghosts 25–6, 31
Silver Seraph 12, 16, 110, 145–6, 182
Silver Shadow 65–6, 71, 80, 82, 83, 89
Silver Spirit 80, 83–4, 85, 109
Silver Wraith series 89
snobbery 62–3
Speed 8 (Bentley) 188
Spirit of Ecstasy 28–9, 171–2
Springfield cars 39–40
state limousine 186
Staveley Industries 164
Supermarines 41–2, 54
   see also Vickers

T-series 80, 83, 89
tanks 59, 70, 72, 80, 156
Toyota 103, 106
trade unions 101
turbocharged Bentleys 94, 95–6, 97
turbojet engines 60–1
the Twenty (Goshawk engine) 35

USA 38–9, 51, 67

Vickers 8–10, 72, 80–1, 87–8, 98–105, 136–7, 140–9, 163–8
Volkswagen 77–8, 152–3, 158–60, 166–74, 177
   BWM secret discussions 160–2, 164, 171–3
   investment in Bentley 177, 182–3
   Seat subsidiary 83, 152
Volkswagen Group 6–10, 14, 16, 104, 133, 138–9

Wall Street crash 46
Ward, Peter 92, 93, 110, 112–13, 115–16, 120
Werner, Helmut 111, 113, 134–5
Whittle, Frank 59
Woodwark, Chris 124, 142, 164
World War II 57–9
Wraith (final Twenty) 35–6

X5 (BMW) 107